dating, mating, and manhandling

Lauren Frances, Ph. Double D

Founder of the Institute for Romantic Research

 Harmony Books/ New York

dating, mating, and manhandling

manhandling

*The Ornithological
Guide to Men*

Published in the United States by Harmony Books, an imprint of the Crown Publishing
Group, a division of Random House, Inc., New York.
www.crownpublishing.com

Harmony Books is a registered trademark and the Harmony Books colophon is a trademark of Random House, Inc.

Library of Congress Cataloging-in-Publication Data
Frances, Lauren.
Dating, mating, and manhandling : the ornithological guide to men / Lauren
Frances. — 1st ed.
p. cm.
Includes bibliographical references.
1. Dating (Social customs) 2. Mate selection. 3. Man-woman relationships. 4. Man-
woman relationships — Humor. 5. Men — Psychology — Humor.
I. Title.
HQ801.F684 2006
306.73 — dc22   2005028907

ISBN-13: 978-0-307-23804-7
ISBN-10: 0-307-23804-0

Printed in the United States of America

10 9 8 7 6 5 4 3 2 1

First Edition

To any woman who's ready for action . . .
                            and satisfaction!

Hope is the thing with feathers
that perches in the soul
that sings the tune
without the words
and never stops at all.

–Emily Dickinson

acknowledgments

I would like to extend my thanks to:

My darling parents, Barbara and Monroe, true Lovebirds for life

My publisher, Shaye Areheart, for taking this project under her wing

*My literary manager, Alan Nevins, for making sure that this
book took flight*

*My editors, Julia Pastore and the mighty Lucy J. Kim, for tending to
this book so carefully*

*Konstantin Kakanias, for his fabulous illustrations
and marvelous spirit*

James Reilly, for his unfailing psychic support

Nina Meledandri, for her love and friendship

Bob Blumer, for his mentorship and surreal inspiration

David Duvall, for his wickedly wise and wonderful counsel

My expert and well-dressed research team:

Leah Horwitz, Alisa Gichon, David and Matthew Glitzer, Stacy
Altman, Laurie Muslow, Eva Roberts, Kim Light, Kathe Mazur, Co-
rina Rohne, Kate Walsh, Gabrielle Francis, Maggie Rowe, Sascha
Ferguson, Katarina Chikalis, Anne Quin-Harkin, Terry Sweeney,

Lanier Laney, Anne Beatts, Kara Kassuba, Andrea Abbate, Penna Omega, Heidi Clements, Courtenay Raia Grean, Ph.D., Andrew Lang, Lisa Ullman, Tommy Lee, Scott Humphrey, Mie Kaneda, Lynn Rosen, Marilee Albert, Joel Michaely, Abdi Nazemian, Jaclyn Laffer, John Markus, Rana Joy Glickman, Robert Barr, Kim Meisner, Andy Galker, Jon Phillips, Gary Shapiro, Marc Segal, the Moss family, Sarah Cartwright, Pamela Ezell, Kate Kennedy, Sibylle Kazeroid, Leta Evanthes, the Micalzos, the Holy Cow, Dale Brasel, everyone at *Flaunt* magazine, and the Godmothers: Blanche Weinberg, Anne Goldsmith, Fredda Issacson, and Pat Segal

All of the specimens who participated in this important research.

And last but not least . . .

. . . to my blond dog, Penelope, for patiently sitting on my lap and at my feet whilst I spent many long hours furiously typing away. Let's go to the dog park!

contents

part ii: mating

Introduction

It has often been said that men are dogs. Any dog owner will be quick to point out the obvious flaw in this unfair comparison. Although men do indeed act like "horn dogs" and "dirty dogs," this refers to their love of recreational sex and their willingness to engage in it anywhere, anytime — even in the middle of the road.

But sadly, the analogy stops there.

Dogs are *remarkably* easy to train. This is clearly not true of most men. Trying to get them to put down a toilet seat can take a lifetime of training. Simple tricks, like foreplay and cuddling, can be magically *un*learned at any time. Canines are loyal for life. They don't have intimacy issues. In fact, the only peace you'll ever get from your furry friend will be when he finally rests in peace.

No, men are not like dogs.
They are, however, remarkably like birds!

My hands-on research has proven time and again that men are like wild things. They startle easily when you make fast moves. They'll often get very, very close to you and suddenly fly away again. When threatened, they may even become hostile or passive-aggressive and flee in an attempt to resist (emotional) arrest.

So following in the footsteps of Jane Goodall, I packed my lingerie and spent quality time in the dating wilds studying these fascinating creatures. After some painstaking (but deeply gratifying) research in the field, I've finally decoded the mating rituals of the Easily Startled

Modern Male. This book clarifies their complex mating behaviors and includes effective manhandling techniques that every woman out of a training bra will *definitely* want to learn. This information will be invaluable when looking for a husband, a boyfriend, or a plaything.

I do realize that in the past, you or a happily married girlfriend may have lucked into the *perfect* relationship, or a *perfect* dating scenario. But now that you're back in the field, you don't have to count on luck. You can count on yourself. This book will show you how.

Read on and learn why:

1. The only person who can ever really waste your time is you!

2. It's not *who* you've been dating but *how* you've been dating that's actually the problem.

3. If you keep doing what you're doing, you'll just keep getting what you're getting.

If you're thoroughly satisfied with what you've been getting, please e-mail your findings to me! (But you're probably too busy having mind-blowing sex or planning your wedding to find the time to read this book.) For the rest of you . . .

Remember: You are now a valued member of my expert and well-dressed research team. This research is important, so really do your homework. You'll need an open mind, a committed heart, and some lip gloss.

Your mission: As a Romantic Researcher, you'll collect data while following specific, step-by-step instructions outlining the most effective ways to conduct each fun field experiment. You won't be out there "winging it" on your own anymore but will learn *exactly* how to approach the objects of your desire and engage them engagingly.

Once you start using these tools, you'll take charge of your romantic destiny and discover that:

1. Dating isn't a mini-relationship, it's a pleasurable fact-finding mission.

2. Until he says he's the One . . . *he isn't!*

3. Dating will always result in the survival of the fittest when you wisely follow the laws of natural selection.

The good news is . . .

Help is on the way! If you're trapped in a romantic bog, or lost in the dark forest of singleness, fear not. In no time you'll wind up in a charming meadow, bathed in glorious sunlight and surrounded by the lovely chirping of birds. Now let's get you out of the woods so you can find your prince. 'Cause after all, *every* girl deserves to have a very sweaty, hot-and-heavy happy ending!

Let's go birding.

Wherever there are people there are birds, so it makes comparatively little difference where you live, if you are only in earnest about getting to know your feathered neighbors.

–Florence A. Merriam

dating

part i

I can never make up my mind which one of you boys is the handsomest! I was awake all last night trying to figure it out.

−Scarlett O'Hara, *Gone With the Wind*

one

Get Flocked

Discovering the Fundamentals of Flirting

I was eleven and watching *Gone With the Wind*. I sported braces, freckles, and octagonal glasses. Mesmerized, I watched as Scarlett O'Hara clung to her bedpost as she was laced into her terrifically tiny corset. Then Atlanta burned and she survived the Civil War and made a fetching green dress from her living room drapes.

But it was the picnic scene at the Hamiltons' that would etch itself forever into my impressionable mind. There Scarlett stood, hooped-out and surrounded by a *huge* flock of men. And as she basked in the center of all that fabulous male attention, she looked just like the cat that ate the canary!

"Now how on earth did she manage that?" eleven-year-old me marveled. It would take some years before I would fully understand her man-catching secret.

Scarlett Deconstructed

Scarlett O'Hara possessed the mind-set of Flock Consciousness. By not focusing exclusively on any one suitor, she lured an entire flock of Lovebirds, and wisely kept her options open. Scarlett was flirtatiously multitasking!

She had every boy at Twelve Oaks eating out of the palm of her hand. *"Why yes, Mr. Hamilton, I'd love some more lemonade, with lots and lots of chipped ice.*" And she needed it because she was on *fire.*

Several years later, braces off and contacts in, I donned a halter-top and a little too much Bonne Bell blush and went to my first high school party. I intuitively practiced what Scarlett had taught me and allowed a flock of boys to gather around without making the silly mistake of getting romantic tunnel vision.

This would land me a date with Paul, the star quarterback, his scent an intoxicating blend of Ivory soap and cigarettes. And also Ross, a towheaded junior who walked me home the next day after soccer practice. His dazzling white teeth would leave a small hickey that my mother would notice and ground me for later that weekend.

My romantic career had officially begun!

What's Good for the Goose
Is Good for the Gander

The most common mistake single women make is to prematurely take themselves off the market simply because "someone likes them" (otherwise known as the *One-at-a-Time Man Plan*).

This misstep can happen during any phase of dating, and is a genetic holdover from the millions of years that women spent picking berries on the tundra. It makes us want to quickly give up the hunt and become "instantaneously monogamous" to a viable suitor once he's been found.

WARNING: The problem is that most men like to date women exactly the other way around.

MAN FACT: *Men, even the ones you think are really nice guys (like architects) believe that it's not only normal, but actually **preferable**, to have several sexual options (women) waiting for them in the wings.*

Men don't think that this approach is wrong as long as they haven't stepped up and made a verbal commitment to any, some, or all of these women. On the contrary, most men subscribe to the **Male String Theory of Dating.**

The Male String Theory of Dating

Boys were learning much more than teamwork in Little League. They also learned the value of rotating the talent. When little boys grow up and become men, they'll apply this principle to their love lives, too. It's ingenious when you understand how it works . . .

A single male has his starting lineup of MVPs, then his Second String Girls, who like him just a little more than he likes them, and finally his Romantic Replacements, who are kept in a holding pattern on the bench.

His MVPs are usually the women he thinks he'll have mind-blowing sex with. The rest are put into romantic rotation.

Men don't feel one shred of guilt about it because, after all, they're not married, so they don't have to act like they are. Maybe they have a point!

The Male String Theory of Dating hinges upon the "If you're dumb enough not to ask me, I'm not gonna be stupid enough to tell you" policy.

Sidebar: It's amazing that more women don't ask the men they're dating if they're currently sexually involved with other women, or how many! If they did, they'd be shocked by the answer.

ROMANTIC RULE: *It's not prying or rude to ask the men you're sleeping with about the competition you're up against, to find out the real odds of contracting STDs—or actual commitments—from them.*

The Solution!

The only way you'll find the right man is if you feel confident rejecting the *wrong* men fearlessly. When you're clear about your needs and know how to communicate and commit to them, you'll quickly assess the real value of the men who court you, and free yourself from the ones who need to be dropped from your flock.

The Good News: If you're one of the MILLIONS of women who've been lulled into thinking that you'll get what you want by passively wishing and waiting, or by throwing terrible fits, this is your lucky day.

ROMANTIC RULE: *Unless men take themselves out of the field for you, don't take yourself out of the game for them!*

Please put your hand over your heart, slip into your sexiest stilettos, and repeat after me:

The Romantic Researcher's Hippocratic Oath

I vow to never again give the precious gift of my exclusivity to any man, no matter how rich or how hot, until he steps up and offers me the kind of relationship that I truly want. Until then, I'll be free to fly at the apex of my own flock of suitors. They'll naturally fall into a pecking order over time, until one day I notice that someone has been happily flying right beside me, with no intention of flying south without me, and I'll have found my lovebird after all!

Now grab your keys and follow me. Let's get flocked!

two

The Art of Flirting

Picking up whomever you want, whenever you want, can be daunting without some basic training under your garter belt. Fortunately, the art of flirting can be mastered by the prepared researcher anytime, anyplace, and can quickly transform you into the man magnet that the Goddess intended you to be.

Solo Birding

The miracle of online dating has been a major boon for single women everywhere. It allows you to shop for men the same way you'd locate Prada at a Barneys sale — with focus and intensity. Although many couples do meet this way, women frequently complain that dot-com men are sometimes slightly irregular, or so unappealing that no one else wants them, either. Quite often the merchandise is *totally* mislabeled. A man will insist it's an XL when it's actually quite small! Or a woman can waste several weeks flirting with an old Coot passing himself off as a jaunty Bluejay, until she finally meets the fiendish fibber in person.

That's why any woman who's serious about birding should learn to proactively flirt with all of the men who are in her *physical* space, as well as in cyberspace. Once you learn how to feed the birds flirtatiously, you'll never again pass up the dashing men who are right under your nose and dying to say hello, at the car wash . . . your vet's . . . and the local Laundromat. Flirting beats flipping through *Cat Fancy* magazine, I promise you that!

Are You a Fantastic Flirt?

No matter how much time you spend outdoors, it will come to no avail if you're still using come-hither techniques that were in vogue sometime around the invention of the maxipad. The following quiz reveals if you're relying on antiquated maneuvers favored by medieval maidens-in-waiting.

Flirt Technique Diagnostic

Are the following statements true or false? Pencils up, and begin.

	TRUE	FALSE
If a woman makes the first move, she'll never know if a man really likes her or not.	—	—
If a woman initiates a first date, a man will automatically think she's looking for sex and won't respect her.	—	—
Men don't like to be asked out by women. They find it emasculating and a turnoff.	—	—

Pencils down, please.

If you answered "True" to all of these questions, you're probably so demoralized by your lack of action that you've stopped bikini waxing!

If eating frozen yogurt is your idea of fun on a Saturday night, your salvation has finally come, hon.

MAN FACT: *There is no man shortage. Your dating technique needs an upgrade.*

Are You Flirting Like You're in a Coma?

Although modern women may not be consciously aware of it, most of us have never quite forgotten, or recovered from, the romantic coaching that we received (and often still believe) from the Brothers Grimm.

These tall tales are the cause for much of the dysfunctional, dating-disordered madness affecting most women today: the belief that finding true love should be just like a fairy tale — some magical event that requires absolutely no effort on your part whatsoever. Instead, it should feel like it's been preordained by some romantic superpower, and it'll happen if it's *s'posed* to, regardless of anything you do. In fact, doing anything about it would seem kind of desperate, and just a little, well, *tacky.*

Now, let's review this for a moment together, shall we?

Once upon a time you were hanging at home in your sweats when suddenly, there was a knock on the door and . . .

Okay, I forgive any woman for getting completely sucked in by this. What woman could possibly refuse a hot prince in leotards who's bearing a gift of *marvelous* shoes? I can barely resist having sex with the Italian shoe salesmen in the stockroom at Barneys when I'm *paying* for them.

Unfortunately, acting like Sleeping Beauty in a Coma (waiting for a prince to rush in and rescue you from a life of intense boredom) is a very bad man plan. There is no data to support the idea that taking long naps and spinning flax will improve your social life whatsoever.

This way of dating — by divine intervention — seems like a good idea until I remember that, unlike Beauty, my fairy godmothers aren't casting love spells to ensure that my romantic fate will survive PMS and other acts of God.

They are at a gay bar.

And there's another big reason these tall tales are so very Grimm.

ROMANTIC RULE: *When you flirt like a medieval maiden you'll wind up spinning your wheels, and the only prick that you'll feel will be easily averted by a thimble!*

The Moral of the Story: In truth, the only things that most of us were paying attention to were the happy ending and the fabulous empire-waist gowns . . . *we just forgot to read the fine print.*

What we should have really learned from these tall tales is that there is a happy ending waiting for any woman willing to endure a little pain, alone time, self-doubt, strange companions, bizarre circumstances, and unforeseen setbacks on the way to her wedding. And some proactive flirting won't hurt you any, either.

Throw 'Em a Crumb

Most single women complain that they don't date enough, but when I ask them how many men they've asked out lately, the answer is often a shocked and confused "None!"

(Nun, get it?)

ROMANTIC RULE: *If you want to go on more dates, ask and ye shall receive, sayeth the bored.*

You can trade in your chastity belt for a garter belt and date as much as you want to, whenever you want to, when you flirt like a self-assured Romantic Researcher, and not like a girl.

Now before I share maneuvers guaranteed to get you working your lingerie drawer, you'll need to trash some old ideas first. Here are two man-catching techniques as current as the crossbow and sure to keep your love life in a *very* deep sleep.

1. R.E.M.ing for romance. Many date-free women are still trying to lure men by using Retinal Morse Code, a series of rapid eye movements, stares, and eyelash battings that signal you're there for the taking but wouldn't dream of doing the asking. This kind of passive flirting is unattractive and makes you look like you have a nervous tic. It's obviously a relic from an earlier time when women didn't have access to mascara.

2. *Being a Size Queen*. Millions of women spend gorgeous weekends on the StairMaster hoping that their dream man will magically appear the very second they can fit back into their skinny jeans. These women blame the size of their thighs for their singleness, and believe that when they finally look perfect, the Barbie Dream House will become theirs, along with Ken and all of those *fabulous* shoes!

I'll let you in on a secret. Even women who are perfect size 4's are often date-free too!

That's why *every* woman, no matter how small or how tall, will benefit from acquiring modern flirting technology.

WARNING: If you continue reading this book, you won't be able to gripe about being date-free ever again!

Feed the Birds

You can date as much as you want to, *whenever* you want to, by mastering the art of the magical phrase *"Nice tie!"*

This maneuver can be performed by the solo birder anytime, any place, and is guaranteed to transform you into the man magnet that the Goddess intended you to be!

How to Become a
Magical Man Magnet

The next time that a man who intrigues you crosses your path, simply compliment something he's wearing or doing. All men love to be admired. They are totally motivated by it, will go to war for it, and build skyscrapers for it, so all you have to do is use this male character trait to your advantage.

Casting a small crumb of approval a man's way will have an amazing "open sesame" effect on him. He will happily chirp away with any woman smart enough to notice his fine feathers . . . and waterproof sports watch.

MAN FACT: *Men are externally referenced. They cuddle up with magazines about breasts, cars, and guns. Conversing with men about any gizmo or inanimate object is always the best way to draw them out.*

WARNING: Never compliment a man on his physique! This will only serve to embarrass or confuse him about what your intentions are. Unless he's twenty-two. Then we know what they are, so go right ahead and spell it out for him!

The secret to breaking the ice is to make sure that your compliment is always once removed. (Exceptions: tattoos and huge biceps. They fall under the purview of man jewelry, too.)

TRUE STORY: I once said, "Nice tie" to a gorgeous man on the red carpet at a film premiere. He whipped it off and proudly handed it to me, to the amazement of his little entourage. *(I used it to tie him to my bedpost one rainy evening . . . but I'll tell you that story later.)*

MANHANDLING MANEUVER: *The best way to break the ice with any man is to quickly pay him a compliment!*

Luring Your Lovebird

After you've engaged a man in light conversation about his car, sneakers, or tie, he may spontaneously ask for your phone number. But what if he's flapping around a bit and isn't confident about coming in for a landing?

WARNING: Only proceed if your first compliment was snapped right up. If it was, throw him this crumb.

"Would you like to get a cup of tea sometime?"

Now before you get your knickers in a twist, consider this . . .

Meeting for tea is very low risk because your intentions are vague.

You aren't asking him to meet you at a strip club. You aren't even asking him to meet you for a drink! You're inviting him to have a proper cup of tea, like any Victorian woman absolutely would. He'll quickly jump to the conclusion that you are (a) a lady and (b) fascinating!

I guarantee that no woman has *ever* asked him out for a cup of tea before. It will make him feel a little confused (this is good) and all sparkly inside.

ROMANTIC RULE: *Don't ever ask a man out for a drink, lunch, or dinner. It's presumptuous and will only put you at a dating disadvantage later. Always leave it to your man to upgrade a teatime request.*

If he hesitates at all, you can easily back up by breezily saying, "Let's get together as friends; it doesn't have to be a tea date per se." This will take all of the pressure off both of you and prevent him from getting cocky.

If your Lovebird's been following the trail of bread crumbs you've been tossing his way, he'll cheerily hop a little closer and chirp, "That'd be great!" This is your cue to say, in the most offhanded way, "Do you have a card, Bernard?"

There are only three possible responses to this question:

1. Yes. He quickly hands his card over. Men will often ask you for your number at this time as well, et voilà! You get a Manhandling Gold Star. And he does, too.

2. Let me get a pen! He doesn't have a card, but leaps at the opportunity to see you again and scrounges up a pen. You now have him eating out of the palm of your hand. Brightly say, "Great, I'll give you a call, Paul."

Caution: Always be vague about when you'll be calling him. *Never* try to set up a date with a man at this time unless he instigates it. Just tuck his number into your purse and smile. This is a *rule*.

Or . . .

3. He turns tail and disengages before doing so. This almost never happens, but if it does, don't fret. And don't push. Just let him fly away. It's of no consequence to you. It simply means that you look like his hot bipolar ex-girlfriend who ruined his life when she went off her meds, or that he's already been banded (*married*). You won't ever know the reason why he let you slip through his fingers, and quite frankly, we don't want to know. Just say, while quickly gliding away: "It was a delight to meet you, André. Have a fabulous day."

MANHANDLING MANEUVER: *If your subject 'fesses up and says he's currently involved with someone, never be embarrassed that you flattered him with your attention. Things couldn't have gotten to this stage unless he was flirting right back at you! It's actually his fault that you're both in this predicament and he's offering an explanation as a way of eating crow. Just say, "Lucky girl!" and smile, while looking him dead in the eye. Consider it a moment of triumph, and then immediately exit stage left.*

WARNING: If a banded or already "tagged" male tries to set up a date with you at this juncture, don't accept! You'll incur *incredibly bad dating karma* if you do. If you entertain these kinds of invitations, or worse, encourage them, call me immediately. You need a little psychic tune-up. I'll probably be out in the field, but I do have a very soothing outgoing message on my answering machine. Please do not leave a message.

Any Questions?

Q: Why should I ask a man out? I want a guy who has enough balls to ask me out.

A: Well, I wish the ice caps weren't melting, but they are. In a perfect world, things would be, well, perfect. But in the real world, men are distracted, rumpled, in terrible need of a shave . . . and sometimes a nudge. According to *Cosmo* magazine, 78 percent of men polled said they loved it when women made the first moves, and didn't think any less of the women who made them. So there you have it. I rest my case.

Okay? Any more questions?

Q: But won't he think I'm a slut if I ask him out for tea?

A: He'll think you're a slut if you *act* like a slut. No one is asking you to behave like one, so don't unless you really *want* to!

HISTORICAL FACT: *Manolo Blahnik (aka God) once said, "I love sluts. They are the kindest people in the world." And obviously quite well-heeled, too.*

Oh, all right, one more question. You there . . . in the back?

Q: *Maybe the Universe doesn't want me to be with anyone. If it does, I'm sure someone will come along, won't they?*

A: Wow, the Universe, although extremely busy, just sent me this note to pass along to you.

Dear Needing a Sign,

We, the Universal Powers That Be, want you to be wildly happy and sexually fulfilled. But we're extremely busy managing black holes and DNA strands and trying to ensure that most of you keep driving on the right side of the road. So we'd really appreciate it if you took the lead in your personal fulfillment; but we do promise to send little clues when you're on the right track — and small, unexpected shoves in the right direction — and we, the Universe, promise to cry at your wedding.

Signed,
The Universal Powers That Be
(very interested in you!)

three

Assembling Your Mantrap Pack

It's now time to organize a "birding party," or what we at the Institute refer to as a Mantrap Pack. Besides being effective, group flirting can be as much fun as lingerie shopping!

Your task: assisting one another while spotting, luring, and capturing prospective Lovebirds. Now that you have my flirting technology at your fingertips, you can get flocked absolutely anywhere, anytime, *together*!

Note: Always remember that you're on a mission. Your happiness and future fulfillment may hang in the balance. I've witnessed hundreds of relationships and marriages resulting from this kind of fieldwork. Stay alert, flirters!

Casting Your Mantrap Pack

Size matters. (But you already knew that!) The ideal number is four because it's perfect for splitting up and double-teaming. *Never* go birding with five or more women, however. This amount of estrogen is too unwieldy and will turn your expedition into a vivacious girls' night out.

Good casting is essential. Begin by asking your most man-motivated girlfriends if they would like to become part of your "expert and well-dressed research team." *Clue:* This should be met with an enthusiastic "Hell, yeah!"

Top-drawer candidates for a Mantrap Pack are supportive and available for consistent and ongoing fieldwork. Needless to say, you'll only want to invite a true-blue Girls' Girl into a birding group.*

A *Note to New Team Leaders:* Not every woman is ideally suited for this task. Try as you will, experience is always the best teacher. You'll find your casting has gone awry if you observe the following:

The Man Hater. She creates a psychic No-Fly Zone that blocks handsome men from approaching and entering your airspace because of her terrifically bad vibe. Men can spot a Man

---

* The Girls' Girl knows that although love affairs may be brief, girlfriends are forever. The Girls' Girl would never dream of letting some hot piece of ass ruin your friendship. She would never *ever* bed your boyfriend, even if he was really hot and they were both drunk and left all alone on a beach in Tahiti. Girls' Girls are not full of envy or jealousy, but enjoy tea parties at Starbucks, and have learned how to share their toys. This lady's got your back.

Hater on their radar from miles away and will instinctively back off. She is like romantic kryptonite and can stop any man mid-flight, causing him to plummet to the earth like a stone.

How to diagnose a Man Hater: You lure men in, but she either acts distant and standoffish, tries to pick a fight with them — or begins to argue with you instead! Men will break through this force field of hate if they find you amazingly attractive, but why set up an obstacle course for them to navigate? If you find this saboteur in your midst, demote her lovingly back to girlfriend status and leave her at home with the remote while you're out on the prowl.

You'll also find that your casting went awry if you discover:

The Man Eater. She views romance as a competition and won't mind sleeping with your boyfriend whether she's drunk or sober. After all, if he was *really* into you, he wouldn't be cheating on you, right? The Man Eater is a terrible candidate for a Mantrap Pack. She only pledges allegiance to her own flag. Never engage in threeways with this woman! She'll be delighted to steal your boyfriend.

Private consultation for the Man Eater: If you're a Man Eater, you obviously don't need a Mantrap Pack. You're *already* packing and can use these manhandling tips all by yourself. Just try to wield your power wisely. If you're reading this book, I can only assume that the prospect of world domination has lost some of its glow, and you're ready for a happy ending that lasts longer than three minutes. Hey, you deserve to be happy. Just don't steal everyone else's toys.

And finally, be sure to sidestep . . .

The Dater Player Hater. This little wet blanket thinks that any dating effort is totally *futile*. Although lovely in every other respect, the Dater Player Hater is a black hole of negativity when it comes to the topic of men. She has a mental loop that automatically derails any effort you make to cheer her up about her love life. She would rather be *right* than *happy*. "I would never date anyone I met in a bar," she'll mutter while you're sipping your martini and flirting with two cute men. At a bar! This woman is way too much work. Don't let her torpedo your romantic plans. Just give her Das Boot.

Any Questions?

Q: Do all the members of a Mantrap Pack have to be single?

A: Absolutely not! You can always bring a Decoy. Your team members don't have to be looking for love themselves to be amazingly effective. In fact, a married woman will often volunteer to perform some of the most dangerous flirtatious field ops. She'll go way out on a limb for you because she has nothing to lose. Well, maybe her pride, but she won't really mind because she's already taken (and married women just love to fix up single girls; it almost borders on a sickness!). They're like little suicide bombers of love, with nothing at stake except your happiness.

Now that you've assembled your team, let's put you on the front lines. Ready, aim, fire . . .

four

Sitting Ducks

*The 18 Most Likely Places
to Spot Your Bird*

If you want to find a Bird of Paradise, you probably won't spot him at your local Taco Bell. Serious bird-watchers know that targeted manhunting expeditions increase the odds of landing the Lovebirds that you most desire.

ROMANTIC RULE: *When it comes to manhunting, "winging it" is for the birds.*

Targeted treks are often best done on weekend afternoons in man-rich locations. Adventuresome and dedicated flirters will soon discover that these expeditions yield fabulous results. The key is to travel off the beaten paths used by every other woman in your neighborhood. If you're game enough to leave your comfort zone, however, you'll discover some *amazing* man-catching opportunities.

Upside for Afternoon Birding: Any man who falls for you when you're wearing jeans and a ponytail will be just wild about you when you're "evening fabulous."*

ROMANTIC RULE: *Change your routine and go where the boys are. Improving your male-to-female ratio will always up the odds of romantic success.*

Planning Your Expedition

Round up your Mantrap Pack and then plan your campaign over cocktails by asking each member to specify the birds that she'd most like to target. Organize your outings to accommodate all of you, or you may pair off on specialized jaunts once you declare your birding preferences. A sample mission might include targeting Condors, Penguins, and Bluejays.

Here are some helpful birding terms:

   TARGET BIRDS: Are at the top of your list and the men that you most desire.

   ACCIDENTALS: Are fellows you'd never expect to find in this strange locale, like Orlando Bloom at the grocery store.

---

* This is taken from studies we conducted on first meetings that led to marriages: 97 percent of the successful birders surveyed remarked, "I was just in my workout clothes!" "I was wearing my sloppy sweater." "I didn't have a stitch of makeup on!" But they were often wearing lip gloss.

NEMESIS BIRDS: Are exasperating Target Birds who keep eluding your grasp even though you're in hot pursuit of them (examples: the Nesting Lovebird, the Homing Pigeon, or the Woodpecker).

Bird Sanctuaries:
The Best Places to Spot Your Bird

The field will be wide open for you here, my dears, and men will be like sitting ducks in your sights!

1. Hardware Stores. These are easy places to strike up a conversation with any man. If one of your Mantrap Pack members likes a fellow who's handy with his tools, go right between the hammers and the nails.

THE UPSIDE: Men you meet at hardware stores already do chores around the house and are often homeowners.

TRUE STORY: I was once looking through paint swatches for my bedroom when a ridiculously good-looking man peered over my shoulder and asked me what color I was leaning toward. "Pink," I replied. "It's the international color of welcome." He laughed and the rest is history (read more in the *Confessions of Dr. L*).

MANHANDLING MANEUVER: Think of something in your home that needs improving, then ask a handsome man to help you find and operate a ratchet, a wrench, duct tape, oh, anything really. And then take the tip and use it!

MAN TACKLE: Always wear high heels at Home Depot. This is a rule.

2. Sporting Events. Men enjoy playing with balls, and love watching other men play with them, too. Stadium games are virtual bird-a-thons, teeming with huge flocks of breeding males who migrate here year-round.

CAVEAT: You must be willing to embrace a relationship that revolves around banners, beer, and barbecues. But you'll know where to find him on Sundays.

THE UPSIDE: Sport birding automatically gives you that Cameron Diaz Factor, even if you're not 5'11", leggy, or blond.

MANTRACK: If you're young and hot and like pro athletes, get a spray-on tan and crash VIP parties celebrating the rare Condors and athletic Master Cocks who have temporarily touched down in your area. Those seriously committed to shagging and bagging this kind of male may even want to try out for the cheerleading squad.

MANHANDLING MANEUVERS:

1. Make frequent trips to the concession stand.
2. Always Google games in advance to pick up valuable sporty tidbits so you won't sound like a total moron while engaged in flirtatious conversations with rabid sports nuts about "the game."
3. Enter a bracket for March Madness basketball with your guy friends. (By the way, betting on a team because you like the looks of their outfits really works.)

3. The Local Basketball Court. It's so fun to watch men playing pickup games *(I mean, really!)* on the weekends. Smart birders come to view the local males strutting their stuff on the neighborhood court.

BONUS: You get to check out their six-packs without having to get naked, too.

MAN TACKLE: Borrow a friend's dog and play fetch near the courts.

MANHANDLING MANEUVER: *Bring an extra bottle of water in case you spot anyone who looks hot when he's sweaty!*

4. Bookstores. These are the perfect places for man-catching, once you know what you're doing. All species of birds convene here—from Horned Owls to Robins. Quickly classify them by observing which section of the store they flock to. This borders on man-catching genius. *(The same rules apply for Blockbuster.)*

MANHANDLING MANEUVER: *Casually stroll right into his aisle and start leafing through books on either side of him, then innocently ask him for a recommendation.*

WARNING: Men who read are often already married so beware of tracking banded Penguins.

5. Watering Holes. Peacocks, Robins, and Bushtits all group together in loose flocks and spend their evenings foraging for women in these intoxicating wetlands. Listen for their drunken *chirrup* as they move from one watering hole to another in pursuit of nighttime fun.

MANHANDLING MANEUVER: *Barhopping is always advised, so plan to do a birding tour of several hot spots per outing. Quick visitations will give you a good idea about which kind of men flock to each watering hole. You can quickly suss out which evenings are best for night birding by asking the waitress. She'll know and tell, so tip her well.*

6. Grocery Stores. Here's another birder's heaven. Go directly to "guy-friendly" food sections. These include, but are not limited to, frozen foods and canned soup aisles, the soda and beer section, bagged chips and treats, and the deli section.

7. **Gun clubs.** Shooting ranges are full of red-tailed Hawks and practicing Republicans. Ask one of these Raptors to help you improve your aim. Or quip: "Is that a Magnum in your pocket or are you just glad to see me?" Bull's-eye!

8. **The gym and beyond.** A variety of species converge at the local gym and produce a spectacular dawn chorus. Go birding early in the morning and see who's motivated enough to buff up before work.

THE UPSIDE: These early birds have jobs. If you go to the pool, you can check out the merch because they'll be almost naked.

TIP: Also check out other man-heavy workout destinations, like boxing gyms and martial arts classes. Unless you want to take up these activities for your health, ask the manager if you can observe the class before you join, so you won't break a nail or your piggy bank while checking out the talent.

WARNING: Many metrosexual males are now flocking to yoga and Pilates mat classes, too. At least they're flexible . . . and smart. Notice how Yoga Boy is throwing the odds in his favor by invading the henhouse. *(Beware of falling for a Pink Flamingo!)*

9. **Sports Bars and Billiard Parlors.** Dodos and Woodpeckers will compete for your attention at the pool table's edge. Full of raucous chirping and crowing, the sports bar is a perfect target destina-

tion for a fun Mantrap expedition. Robin Redbreasts, Larks, and Homing Pigeons will be in full view, too.

TIP: Find out the dates and times of big games well in advance to make sure it's worth the trek.

MAN TACKLE: Only slow dancing with a stranger is sexier than having him watch you work a big *(cue)* stick.

10. Men's Department Stores. Men are often dazed and confused in this locale and are often found waddling around, totally lost. Peer through the dense *(clothing)* cover to spot him. Stay alert. He may be a rare find and well worth the effort.

MANHANDLING MANEUVER: *Ask him for help! Say: "You look like you're the same size as my brother. Would you mind trying this on?" or "Do you like this cologne? I can't tell if it's man-friendly."*

11. The Apple Store. This place is always teeming with men, men, men, looking for gadgets and gizmos, gizmos and gadgets. I once spotted Tommy Lee here. Ask one of these potential Lovebirds for help. He may be as confused as you are, but he'll pretend not to be. Cute!

12. Driving Ranges and Tennis or Squash Courts. These locales are full of Bluebirds and Arctic Terns.

MANHANDLING MANEUVER: *Ask some lucky fella to help you improve your stroke.*

MAN TACKLE: Wear something asstastic! *(If you're wearing white, remember to self-tan.)*

13. *Fund-raisers.* These events provide reliable birding for some of the most desirable and otherwise hard-to-find Condors, Dominant Crowing Cocks, and Pterodactyls, who are commonplace sightings in this locale.

MAN TACKLE: Wearing vintage Halston while man-trapping is tons of fun! Make sure a Pink Flamingo helps you accessorize.

14. *Singles Events/Pro Matchmaking Services/Club Med.* Birding tours like Club Med can take you all over the world and allow you to have fun flings, with tropical Birds of Paradise and Toucans, or get pursued in earnest by Sparrows and Homing Pigeons. *(Even Herring Gulls look sexy in an exotic locale!)* Local singles events are advertised in newspapers, and online, and attract flocks of single men, too. You might even hire a professional matchmaker who'll act as a bird guide. Matchmakers charge for their services but are often worth every penny.

15. *The Beach.* Shorebirds of all types flock here in droves. July is the month to watch for the juveniles and adult males of all breeding species.

WARNING: It's often harder to identify a bird without his plumage *(clothing).* This can be a confusing time for bird-watchers, as many young males may look like another species altogether!

MANHANDLING MANEUVER: *Undo your bikini top and say, "Can you pass me the sunblock? Ohhh, I can't reach my back . . . can you help?"*

16. *Strip Clubs.* Bring your binoculars while birding in this classic male sanctuary *(wear a pink wig).* Almost anything is liable to turn up here, from irked Homing Pigeons and Sparrows, to the common

Bushtit and a stunning variety of Dirty Birds. If you're game enough to go into deep cover and perform your surveillance from the inside, you will find them congregated at the catwalk's edge. Ask your male friends to escort you into, *and then out of,* the cathouse!

CAVEAT: He'll want a woman who works the pole.

MANHANDLING MANEUVER: *Say, "Do you have change for a ten?"*

17. Comic book conventions. These events are teeming with men. If nerds set your heart on fire, these conventions are your best shot. He may be be wearing a costume when you meet him, but who am I to judge?

MAN TACKLE: Dress like Wonder Woman and they'll flock to you in droves!

18. Events, Expos, Lectures, Classes and Tournaments. Bowling and fly-fishing tournaments, the local rodeo, heavy metal reunions, big-rig racing, demolition derbies, extreme sports competitions, science lectures, money market and investment seminars, automotive expos . . .

You get the idea. Grab your local paper and look for listings of events that you would *never* have thought of attending. Who knows? You might just wind up with a passion for restoring vintage cars and snag yourself a hot boyfriend, too.

When you go on targeted dating treks with your Mantrap Pack, you'll soon have a lively flock teeming all about you.

Remember to record your bird sightings. You might want to keep a diary to list the birds you see in your yard, in your town, or on your vacation. Flirt your butt(s) off and have tons of fun hunting men in their natural habitats!

five

Flirting in the Field

The following field maneuvers can be used by your Mantrap Pack, and when you're flirting solo, too! They're guaranteed to increase your confidence in the field and fill out your fine flock. Once you practice them several times, they'll become second nature to you. Working the field is so much fun once you learn how to lure the men in your sights who are circling you.

Flirtatious Field Maneuvers

Get a bird's-eye view of the room. I cannot stress the importance of using this time-saving technique enough. Climb directly to the highest vantage point in any venue and position yourself at the top of the stairs or at the railing of a balcony to quickly survey the terrain and assess the talent. (You can even use a pair of small opera glasses, like women used to do!) If you're at a concert, walk right up to the stage and then turn around, et voilà! The entire room will now be facing you. A good lookout can quickly turn any advantageous vantage point to her advantage.

Never sit with your back to a room. You won't meet them if you can't greet them, so always position your Pack to easily spot incoming men. *Never* place yourself in a secluded or quiet area of a bar or restaurant. Instead, position yourself in high-traffic areas by requesting a table or barstool close to the front-line action.

Keep exploring. If you're at a club or an event and it's a dud, skip out and move on to the next. Hey, that's why they call it going on a Manhunt! Always coordinate your team's itinerary and plan at least three man-friendly destinations to explore per mission.

Peer about. You can always pretend to be looking for someone. (You are! You just haven't found him yet.) Begin at one corner of a room and then do a lap around the perimeter. If you're in a crowded venue, do this every twenty minutes.

Scout them out. One of you should volunteer to play the role of Scout. Scouts keep tabs on exotic birds on the move and perform covert operations that provide valuable intel for what would otherwise soon turn into romantic suicide missions. Scouts do a quick lap around the room, and then immediately return and give a field report: "Forget it, babe. He's making out with some girl at the bar."

Don't forget high-volume areas. Lobbies are excellent places to mantrap, and are commonly overlooked by the inexperienced flirter. Since the advent of no-smoking laws, designated smoking sections can often be more fun to flit through than the bars themselves (unless you have asthma!).

Falconing

You can attract birds to your nest with just a little work by using the **Come-Hither Hand Signal**®, my patented man-magnet system. This gesture is guaranteed to penetrate across any crowded room and right into the heart of even the most intimidating man cluster.

MANHANDLING MANEUVER: *The Come-Hither Hand Signal*®

The Lure: Command him invitingly. Get a handsome man in your sights. Look him straight in the eye, while crooking your finger in a come-hither motion and giving him a tiny smile. Men find this gesture irresistible because it's utterly sexy and confident; they will fly to you like Falcons.

The Bait: When he lands at your side, say, "Nice tie! This is my girl-friend Courtney."

The Handoff: Turn to your grateful girlfriend and say, "I'm going to go find Stacy. I'll be back in a minute." (And smile.)

Then Take Off: Now leave the two of them alone. They can simply exchange pleasantries and then drift apart if they don't connect. But if they do, good for you!

You can always use the Come-Hither Hand Signal to lure men directly to your side, too. Although this might sound daunting, it's actually quite fun and so easy to do, and excellent training for the inner dominatrix in you!

Playerette Positions and Love Life–Saving Activities

The following Playerette Positions are tactical maneuvers that can only be accomplished by a smooth-running unit. After just a little practice, the results will be stunning.

1: Mantrap Pack Migration

Some Lame Duck keeps orbiting your Mantrap Pack and is managing to cock-block other males you'd much rather give clearance to. This situation was quickly remedied by a savvy Los Angeles–based Mantrap Pack.

Case Study

We noticed an undesirable tracking us but we just couldn't shake him off our tail. He kept eavesdropping and performing unwanted surveillance. We followed standard protocol and performed a *Mantrap Pack Migration* (positional relocation to the other side of the bar), but this turkey kept up in very unhot pursuit. So we went right into Plan B.

Plan B: I turned to him and said, "We're having a private conversation. Have a good night," and then we swiftly turned our backs on him.

Unfortunately he was a cling-on, so I said, with energy, "Dude, you're blocking traffic. We aren't interested! Good night." It got our team dweeb-free immediately.

2: The Human Shield
Case Study

Our pack was at a concert one night when our scout, Leah, spotted a very hot Swede smiling at her. She also spied another girl desperately trying to get his attention. She quickly gave the verbal signal, "Mascara!" and we swiftly repositioned ourselves to block the visual sight path between her target and the interloper.

Target His Wingmen. Then, our Mantrap Pack quickly circled the wagons by using the magical phrase "Nice extreme sportswear!" to distract his wingmen.

Divide and Conquer. Soon the rest of us were chatting up his friends. They were gorgeous, too! Sometimes being selfless really is its own reward! This left the sexy Swede free, and Leah stepped right in . . . much to his delight.

So what happened next?

They hit it off and wound up dating for three steamy weeks before Sven had to venture forth to another extreme surfing event in Bali. I'm happy to report that before he left, he definitely waxed her board!

Excellent work, ladies, and thanks for the report.

ROMANTIC RULE: *Never allow Lame Ducks to prevent your target birds from entering your airspace. Always shoot down the pests, and keep your landing strip free and clear. (This goes for bikini waxing, too, my dear.)*

six

Get Your Ducks in a Row

If a man has taken your phone number, but he's also managed to slip you his, you must always wait for him to call *you*. Period. If you wound up with his card, however, you're in luck. Read on and discover exactly how to make this little windfall work for you.

After every birding outing, deposit all of your collections *(phone numbers)* into a sterile container *(card file)*. You can wave a little wand over it several times and say, "May there be a Lovebird among these toads." Then let him incubate for four days before deigning to give him a ring.

Why four days? you might ask. Why not two days, or even three? If you're wondering if this rule is a whim, let me assure you that all of my information is based on the most up-to-date romantic research. Check out these results from the latest *Maxim* poll . . .

How Long Should a Guy Wait to Call a Girl After Getting Her Number?

One day _____   A week _____

Two days _____   More than a week _____

Three days _____

Answer

One day: 44%

Two days: 42%

MAN FACT: *The two-day callback rule is for men only. They expect you to call them within three days because that's exactly what they'd do.*

Many women botch a perfectly good opportunity to mantrap because they use this male mating technique. While you may always mirror a man's level of interest, *never* mimic his calling pattern. We want to create intrigue, not predictability.

Now, curiosity may have killed the cat, but it's totally purrrfect for bird hunting. So take away his cocksureness and create some mystery by giving him just enough time to wonder whether you lost his number, were pulling his leg, or have forgotten about him altogether. Congratulations! You have become elusive, a prize, and have potentially magnetized him to you.

You have just created:

INTRIGUE *n* 1. an involved plot to achieve your ends. 2. a clandestine love affair with a hot man in a foreign country who says things to you in bed that you don't understand, but like! *v* 3. cause him to be terribly interested in you.

Call him on day four between 2 and 5 P.M. It's unwise to call a strange bird in the morning or late at night. Don't intrude on his personal time. Instead, give him a ring midafternoon. He'll be settled back into his work and won't be hungry. (It is always unwise to surprise a man who hasn't eaten, unless you're nude or have access to food.)

Vital Rule: You're only ringing him up to say "hello!" Allow him to ask you for a date if he so chooses.

Now grab the phone . . . then make his day, and dial . . .

Love Script

"*Hey there, Tim. It's Lucy Fur, the girl who you rescued from boredom at the mathematician competition. How are you?*"

Congrats! You've passed him the ball, and he should volley right back. If there's something to make a wry joke about, certainly do.

After about two minutes of pleasant chitchat, end the conversation by saying: "*I've gotta run, but it was so nice speaking with you again, Tim.*"

Now comes the moment of truth.

The Lucky Duck picks right up and is *thrilled* to hear from you. He may even say that he was about to stake out wherever it was that he met you in the hopes of bumping into you again. This happens to all of my research team members constantly. Well done. You've lured yourself a Lovebird! The Lucky Duck won't let you slip through his hands twice and will upgrade your date from tea to something more romantic and substantial, like dinner.

Sometimes, however, we may have accidentally drawn in wingnuts:

The Blackout Drinker seems to have trouble remembering who you are. If, after some brief prompting, he still can't place you, say, "I can't hear you . . . uh-oh . . . sorry, my cell is cutting out!" and quickly hang up. This isn't rude on your part. After all, he flirted with you, gave you his card, and is now pretending that he doesn't remember you. Don't waste one more second on him. This man doesn't need a date, he needs rehab!

The Iceman Cometh. He pleasantly twitters away *without* asking you for your number or trying to set up a date because he's married, and now that he's sober, remorseful.

MAN FACT: *If a man thanks you for calling without making plans to see you, he's a goner.*

Don't waste one more second on him and toss it off. What you're much more likely to hear, however, sounds like this: "Wait! Are you free this weekend? I'd love to see you again."

When you hear this sweet birdsong, you're in the catbird seat!

Birds on the Wire

Always follow these unbreakable rules when you're calling new flock members.

The Cloak of Silence. In the beginning stages of courtship, call males Mondays through Thursdays only. Never call a man you aren't sleeping with on Friday, Saturday, or Sunday, unless he's gay or an accountant.

The Virtual Heaven of *67. If you're nervous, you can use the *67 calling feature to mask your phone number. That way, you can simply hang up and no one will be the wiser.

Chickening Out When Calling Him. Even experienced daters can revert to adolescent behavior and suddenly hang up, otherwise known as the "OHMYGOD" reflex. Don't feel too bad. Grown women everywhere do it. Even in Prague. Call back as soon as you recover, and say, "Hi there, Paul. I tried to leave you a message earlier but got cut off by an incoming call. How are you?"

When to Call Back Your Bird. Only call a man right back if it regards an imminent plan. Otherwise, delay the call for at least several hours, or until the next day. Hey, you have a life! Or you're now going to start acting "as if" and *pretend* that you do.

*69ing. As for *69ing, ignore this calling feature entirely. I don't like to encourage it in the bedroom, either. It's like allowing your man to drive drunk. He needs to be alert to stay in the lane!

Rule: You should be way too busy to worry about random phone numbers that pop up on your telephone. But if someone keeps calling and hanging up, hit *69 and say, "Dr. Klein, is that you? Are my pregnancy test results back?"

CLICK.

VM Interception. Voice-mail Interception can be a real life-saver. If you see his number and your heart turns over because his call comes as a shock, or you're way too crushed-out to talk in complete sentences, call him back when you stop hyperventilating. It's the modern version of fainting.

seven

Male Courtship Displays

The first several dates should be light, fun, and romantic. Your man should pick you up, make reservations, and restrain himself from trying to bone you like a fish. Any deviation from this time-tested formula is always a red flag. A man earns a woman's affection through proper care and consistent attention. On a first date, and *every* date, a man should impress you with his ability to care *for* and *about* you.

MAN FACT: *Men invest in the things they value with the resources they have at their disposal, be it cash, creativity, energy, or enthusiasm.*

Always notice if he's rowing through the air first with one wing and then the other to win your affection, or cruising right along with sails set. If he makes plans that are insultingly casual, doesn't compliment you, and is unaffectionate, it's a clear sign that he's withholding his approval. Take his lackluster performance seriously and shoo him right out of your nest without further ado. You certainly won't miss him.

See Arctic Tern, Mockingbird, and Mute Warbler.

MAN FACT: *The plans that a man makes for you tells you the plans that a man has for you!*

What to Look For

Long lead time. The considerate male always calls well in advance. He knows that you're too in demand to have huge holes in your calendar, and he'll want to make sure to reserve some of this valuable time for himself.

A *Confirming Call.* You should always receive a confirming call before 3 P.M. on D-Day. Enthused and thoughtful men call the day before, and also when they're en route. If there will be any delay, you should be notified well in advance. If he calls after 6 P.M. on D-Day, tell him you would love to see him, but you've just made other plans.

A *Little Planning.* It's always a good sign when a man has made reservations. It's proof that he isn't winging it and can organize himself enough to think about you, make a plan, and then stick to it. Beware the girly-man who asks in a whiny voice what *you'd* like to do. He's either lacking in testosterone or motivation, or he just wants to have sex with you and then quickly move on. Men who don't make reservations *for* you often have reservations *about* you.

MAN FACT: *If a man can't come up with a reservation for you on date day, then you should start having reservations about* him.

If you're wondering who should pick up the check, consider this, Miss:

REALITY CHECK: Women spend wads of money on first dates: there's bikini waxing *(painful)*, manicures and blow-drys *(time-consuming!)*, lingerie *(expensive)*, and Pilates *(ridiculously overpriced)*. It's a serious investment for women to show up for date one. The very least a man can do is pick you up and feed you!

A *Lovebird lands on your doorstop at the appointed time.* It's bad form for a man to keep a woman waiting in general, but especially so on a first date. This often throws me into complete Dressing Disorder. This occurs when your date is so late that you keep changing your clothes until the doorbell rings and are then forced to greet him midoutfit! We blame this on the tardy man, who should've arrived on time to avert this crisis.

TRUE STORY: I once had a date ring my bell twenty-two minutes late, who then eyeballed me and actually had the nerve to say, "Wow, you look like you're ready to perform in an off-Broadway play!"

The upside: I was totally disinclined to allow him into my bedroom, which was now strewn with dresses and shoes.

Now really, if a man can manage to arrive at work on time and plant his ass in front of the TV in time for the play-offs, he can ring your doorbell on time. After all, you're big game, too!

Here's a good rule of thumb: Although men should be on time, women are always allowed to be a little late. They know you have Dressing Disorder, too. Don't you feel better?

I certainly do.

eight

Strutting

In the bird kingdom, the male struts his stuff and displays his fine feathers to get the female's attention. The male mating dance is a highly evolved ritual.

BIRD FACT: *Have you ever wondered why the peacock's tail has so many eyes? It's because he wants to get laid! His girlfriends, aka peahens, are fascinated by the large staring eyes on the tails of their gorgeous suitors. They actually put her into a mild state of hypnosis, making it much easier for the peacock to lunge at her. Therefore, the more eyes he has on his tail, the more irresistible the peahen will find him. It is only logical that peacocks have evolved larger and larger eyes on their tails to exploit her preference. And to get some peahen love.*

The same is true for men. They'll try to seduce you at exotic restaurants, ply you with alcohol, and make up transparent excuses to get you to nip into their mansions after dinner. Male posturing is a mating directive emanating from deep within his reptilian brain, even if he's wearing Gucci.

So all you women in the wild should bear this in mind.

MAN FACT: *A man who isn't trying to impress you isn't very impressed with you.*

Strutting Their Stuff and the Male Need for Approval

When a man goes into "breeding mode," he automatically starts to strut his stuff. He does this by telling you how he *destroyed* the competition at the board meeting, vanquished a Nordic invasion of cross-country skiers in Aspen, or parked his car on the street because he hates to valet. These boasts are displays of his potency and sheer dominance over all other males, *made for your benefit.* In other words, "PICK ME puh-lease."

So never be insulted if a man tries too hard to impress you. Don't confuse his preening for insecurity. He's actually paying you an enormous compliment.

Your male is performing an ancient male courtship ritual for your delight and is so very interested that he's begun flaunting his plumage in a lively display of male prowess and virility. He's letting you know that if you do choose him, you'll be making the right male selection. This boastful crowing is no different from a female who tightens her bra straps to present a little more cleavage. Take it as a feather in your cap and enjoy the show.

If you get bored listening to him sing his own praises, wait till he starts cooing in your ear about how much he loves your gorgeous butt and your beautiful thighs. And then we'll talk.

Always beware, however, of males who flaunt large wads of cash early on. Wealthy men often use money and flash in lieu of real intimacy and heartfelt romance.

ROMANTIC RULE: *Remember, men don't have to drop large bills to make you feel like a goddess. They just have to worship you!*

Love Songs and Seductive Warblings

Men are visual creatures. Compliments to your outfit and physique are the first indication that he is physically attracted to you. When a man doesn't reassure you with this kind of positive attention, it's a real statement . . . *about him.* The very least a man can do is say, "Nice hairdo."

MAN FACT: *A man who is attracted to you will always compliment you.*

Compliment Withholders, aka Mute Warblers. There are some strange birds who stubbornly refuse to give compliments. These men are often so attracted to you that they'll try to take you down a notch or two to even out the playing field. This lack of generosity is the result of their own low self-esteem and indicates a strong tendency to withhold, and *always* foreshadows trouble to come. Peckish Mute Warblers like to be perched right above you and may crap on you at any time.

Another quiet guy to always be on the lookout for is called the **Sweet Mute Warbler.** He simply adores you but is just terribly shy. Although he has difficulty singing your praises, he'll compensate for this deficiency by lavishing you with lots of loving attention. These men often make excellent husbands, so stay alert to the differences between the two types of mutes. Choose the sweet, and not the brute!

Professional Songbirds. (*See* Aviary, The Nightingale.) This smooth-talker is *too* adept at the art of the compliment. Listening to a Nightingale sing your praises is delightful, but don't expect too many repeat performances of his arousing arias, because he's often a skilled womanizer, too.

How to Tell Whether You're Being Wooed or Worked

The key here is in his tone. If the compliments are "You're so beautiful, gorgeous, amazing, pretty, and smart!" he's singing a lovely tune. If, however, his comments are strictly sexual, these aren't compliments at all, but predatory breeding signals alerting you to the fact that he's preparing to come in for the kill. Enjoy the serenade, if you will, but these aren't love songs, my ladies. He's just a Lark.

Check out the line my date used last Saturday night: *"Baby, I want to do bad things to you that I promise you're gonna like."*

I have to admit that he was so right!

Always Let Men Sing Your Praises

When I was nineteen, a handsome Brit stopped me and said, "My, you're pretty!" I giggled and shyly looked away. He tipped my chin up with one finger, and said, "When a man gives you a compliment, always look him in the eyes and say, 'Thank you.'"

I turned beet red but did as he bade me. And then he kissed me. I've never forgotten his advice, or that kiss.

ROMANTIC RULE: *Getting paid a compliment is like receiving a gift. It's only polite to respond with easy grace and a thank-you note.*

Etiquette in the Aviary

nine

First Date Dos and Don'ts

If you adhere to smart birding practices, you'll avoid these potential mishaps without snagging a stocking.

1. Don't get drunk! Always maintain enough sobriety to assess your date's character. If you start doing Jell-O shots, you may accidentally wind up in the backseat of his Explorer with your skirt around your head. Practice restraint, and don't have more than a drink or two when you're out on a first date. Otherwise, how in the world can you possibly observe your bird and discover if he's remotely right for you?

MANHANDLING MANEUVER: *Always stay sober enough to remember how naughty you were the night before!*

2. Don't talk about your personal problems. Therapists get butterflies inside when you talk about alcoholic relatives or how traumatized you are by the number of germs thriving in public restrooms. The typical male, however, will be just horrified. You'll have violated the sacred airspace of "romantic quality time," and these little monologues of strange pain will be as off-putting as sorting unwashed laundry in the restaurant. If you're prone to making this manhandling

51

mistake, you need a therapist, not a boyfriend. Or a boyfriend who's a therapist.

MANHANDLING MANEUVER: *You already know all about you. Keep your problems to yourself and get to know him.*

3. Don't be negative about dating. Why should a man pursue someone who isn't happy? It's ineffective manhandling to dump your dating disappointments on Bachelor Number 3. Complaining about how awful dating is just begs the question "Are you in therapy?"

MANHANDLING MANEUVER: *Be a romantic challenge, not a mental-health challenge.*

4. Don't spook your bird. Don't point out your physical flaws to your lover. Only bring these complaints to people who can actually do something about them, and not to people who are sleeping with you, and who will now be forced to lie to you. Waxers, trainers, manicurists, hairdressers, plastic surgeons, and lingerie salesgirls are among the army of specialists who'll relish discussions about your "problem areas" and dysmorphic-body self-image. But beware: Once you draw your lover's attention to the little mole that you secretly despise, he'll find it impossible to overlook it, too, *forever.* And forever is a *very* long time.

INTERESTING FACT: Elle McPherson was once asked if there was anything about her physique that she would ever change. "I wish I had better nail beds!" she replied. I've never forgotten it, much to my chagrin. I don't want to think about Elle's nail beds, but there it is . . . lodged in my brain *forever,* and now in yours, too. Remember: Confidence is sexy!

MANHANDLING MANEUVER: *Sometimes, thoughts are for the inside.*

5. Don't talk badly about your exes. I don't care if he cheated on you with your sister at your bat mitzvah, never recite a laundry list of grievances about your exes. This will only make you sound unavailable at best, or worse, *wounded.* Reveal your secrets when you're both on a beach in Hawaii, or better yet, engaged. By then, he'll want to tend to your sniffles. And then you can blow him.

MANHANDLING MANEUVER: *We all have baggage. Keep it in the closet on first dates.*

6. Don't cock the gun. If you're a recovering nymphomaniac or if you've sworn off playing the slots, keep it to yourself for now. Based on my research, anyone who's any fun usually has one or two skeletons in their closet. It's unwise, however, to reveal your Achilles' heel to men too soon. When you alert a man about what behaviors won't fly with you, he may sweep a nasty habit or even an addiction right under the rug. If he doesn't run, he'll put on a game face to get you to shag him or, worse, marry him. You'll be stunned when he drains the minibar on your honeymoon and comes home as drunk as a Loon.

MAN FACT: *Men loathe being rejected. It makes them feel bad. Instead, they'd much rather hide any nasty habits that they know you'll disapprove of, so that they can seduce you, and reject you, instead.*

Remember: It's easier breaking things off on date three than year three! Always let your date reveal his sticky wickets without your interference, to quickly gauge his character.

MANHANDLING MANEUVER: *When you reveal your Achilles' heel too soon, you'll wind up shooting yourself in the foot.*

7. Don't chase your bird. Never deprive a man of the thrill of the chase. Besides, it's *so much fun* being caught! A woman can always initiate a first tea date, but after that, it's up to a man to decide whether he really wants to nest. Entice men, play with them, and then release them. Allow men to initiate their forward assault (i.e., moving your relationship forward). When you allow them to pursue *you*, they'll often wind up chasing you right around the bed and straight up the altar!

> *A romance is like an egg.*
> *When you hold on*
> *too tightly, it cracks.*
>
> —Lauren Frances, Ph. DD

MANHANDLING MANEUVER: *When you lure men in, they're less likely to fly away.*

8. Don't keep squawking. Don't feel pressured to fill up every second with meaningless chatter. If the conversation falls silent for a moment, don't panic, just let it happen. Natural pauses are very sexy, and body language can be so much more powerful than words. Slowly smile at him and breathe. You may be surprised when he blurts out in the middle of a deliciously pregnant pause, "Come here and kiss me!"

MANHANDLING MANEUVER: *Sometimes less conversation is more.*

9. Don't lower the tone. It's easy be pleasant when we're enjoying ourselves, but the true test of character is how we behave when we're terribly bored or, worse, treated shabbily. There's nothing to be gained by suffering through a terrible date, so if you're having a gawd-awful time, depart quickly and gracefully, without being rude. When you're itching to leave the aviary, say: "This isn't clicking for me, but thank you so much for meeting me, Jerome. I think it's time for me to go on home." Then smile, and add, "Take care."

Extend your hand for a quick shake, swiftly turn on your heel, and depart.

MANHANDLING MANEUVER: *If you're on date number one and aren't having fun, set him free immediately!*

#350 01-30-2014 3:03PM
Item(s) checked out to Hoornbeek, Linda

TITLE: Dating, mating and manhandling :
BARCODE: 11600020625869mvlp
DUE DATE: 02-20-14

Poudre River PLD & FRCC- Harmony Library
Renewals:221-6740 or poudrelibraries.org

ten

Bewitching Your Bird

Tools of the Trade
for a Great First Date

The most common mistake women tend to make when going on a manhunt is making an unqualified "impulse buy." Most women tend to be far more skilled at selecting the jeans that they purchase than the men that they're willing to try on for size. The most levelheaded lass will often throw caution to the winds when it comes to qualifying a man for the irreplaceable gift of her time, her heart, and possibly her future!

This is why it's vital to perform rigorous romantic research on your subjects from date one. It will ensure that you don't mistake rabid Prairie Chickens for healthy, available men ever again.

A Properly Handled First Date Should Yield the Following Information About Your Bird:

His availability for a relationship right now.

Whether he has problematic "commitment issues."

His values system regarding marriage.

His relationship history.

His relationship goals.

Your probable odds of future happiness with him.

Did I just hear someone in the back of the room make a crack that there's no way to get that much information from any man on a first date (or during an entire relationship, for that matter)?

You're in for a lovely surprise! When you follow this man plan, your date will not only share his innermost secrets with you, he'll enjoy himself while he's doing it, too.

Get in the Catbird Seat

You're on your first date and have just ordered a glass of Perrier. "He's so handsome," you think. "I could really like this man!" Instead of getting led astray by unfocused flirting, now is the purrrfect time to collect data with the following playful queries.

Q: Do you enjoy your work?

This "innocent" question yields tons of useful information about his financial and emotional stability. If he's proud of his status and accomplishments in the workplace, he'll gladly talk about them in great detail. If he's ashamed, he'll quickly duck the question.

*Q: Have you recently cared for something that required air to survive?**

Q: Have you ever had sex with a Republican?

If you're of a strong political bent, it's always wise to find out if you're on the same team. With such a delightful question, he'll let you

---

* Like pets, children, plants, or former spouses. This lets you know if he's dependable and responsible, or if he just likes flying solo.

know exactly where his allegiance lies and what color stripe he's saluting.

Q: *Would you like to thumb wrestle?*

This is a fun way to initiate physical contact with men, and gives you oodles of information about a man's competitive nature. Is he a good sport? Does he let you win? Does he hurt you? Is he confident? Does he have nice hands? Are they big? *Now we're talking.*

These questions should be memorized and asked while performing the next man-magnetizing technique. . . .

Flying in Formation

When you fly in formation with your Lovebird, he'll think that you're birds of a feather!

1. *Play follow the leader.* To get in synch with any man, pretend that he's your flock leader and then begin to mirror his physical posture, body movements, and vocal tempo. This is ridiculously easy to do while eating an appetizer.

Example: You're sitting across from each other over drinks. When he leans in, mirror this movement several seconds later by leaning forward. When he settles back into his chair, slowly lean back. He'll begin to feel open and very relaxed around you.

His inner GPS (Girl Positioning System) will be unimpeded; you are wonderful, it says; you're not crowding his airspace one bit. People who are deeply in love automatically do this without giving it conscious thought. They are just "in tune" with each other because they've been having sex all day!

2. *Parrot his vocal tempo.* Once you're in synch with his movements, listen to his verbal patterns. If he chirps away excitedly, parrot

his upbeat rhythm. If he vocalizes in a more melodious way, answer his call by singing the same seductive tune right back at him.

3. *Breathe in unison.* Follow his breathing pattern by watching his shoulders rise and fall. Males will respond as if hypnotized when you perform this simple yet powerful tantric yogic practice. Once you play follow the leader for a short while, you'll have set the stage to plunge into the depths of his very soul . . .

4. *Ready, aim, fire!* By now you're mirroring his posture, his birdsong, and his breathing pattern, but to fully connect with his heart, you must go one step further. While looking deeply into his eyes, slowly inhale. Try to maintain steady eye contact for several seconds longer than you normally would.

Bonus points! Break eye contact to compose yourself if this gets too intense. You may even find that you laugh a little. Don't be alarmed if you do. This exercise can make even the most jaded woman blush! He'll find this display of feminine surrender charming. He'll think he made it happen to you *all by himself.*

He won't notice that you've been mirroring him, but if he does, he'll think that you're both so in synch that you've responded to his call and are naturally following his lead. He won't really know that *he's* been under your spell, and not the other way around.

"Hmmm, I wonder if she'll follow me into the bedroom."

MAN FACT: *Men love to take credit for everything. This is a perfect opportunity to let them!*

Techniques to Enchant Your Man

Breathe slowly and smile softly. Whenever you become nervous, just breathe slowly and deeply, three times in a row. On the first two breaths, look away, but on the third inhalation, raise your eyes to his face, breathe in and out again, and smile softly. This will drive him wild.

Draw his attention to you. Any languorous movement done deliberately is fascinating. You might try slowly spreading your napkin on your lap and smoothing it down, or slowly drinking from your glass while looking into his eyes, licking your lips, or twirling your hair around your finger. Gestures like this will captivate his attention.

Signal your attraction. Communicate your attraction through tiny affectionate gestures, like touching his sleeve, smiling back at him, or brushing up against him accidentally *(on purpose)*. He'll get the message and respond in kind, by taking your hand, and moving closer to you . . . and closer . . .

Note: Flying in formation works in the courtship phase, and *every subsequent* phase of manhandling. If you ever need to have a relationship "talk," this secret maneuver will unlock his heart and make him far less prone to flying off the handle.

ROMANTIC RULE: *Remember, birds of a feather flock together.*

You're off to a fantastic start, and a date to remember!

Pretty Bird

Now that you have his full attention, let's stroke his fine feathers and start singing his praises.

Failure to admire the men who flock to your side is a common mistake of the inexperienced flirter. Whether your bird is a Condor or a Dove, he'll be watching you like a hawk for telltale signs to see if he can satisfy you. It is as if you are a litmus test of his innate masculinity. He'll want to know that you find him desirable.

ADMIRATION 1. a favorable judgment. 2. feeling aroused by something strange and surprising. 3. "My goodness, you have such big hands. I bet you can open stuck jelly jars with ease!"

MAN FACT: *Men need admiration. It's that simple, people.*

Your date will want to feel capable of filling your bill. If he thinks that it's impossible to impress you, or worse, that you're withholding your approval, he'll flee. He'll want a woman who approves of him and admires him, and who can blame him? This could be why older men prefer to date nineteen-year-olds, but it's only a theory.

MAN FACT: *Men want to be with women who are smart enough to see the best in them.*

If you're a handful (*strong, smart, and sassy*), your bird will be on high alert to see if he can make you happy. The wise manhandler makes it her business to stroke the nervous bird to counteract this tendency. When you learn the art of validating men, they'll feel encouraged, capable of satisfying you, and feel quite affectionate toward you.

Make Him Puff Out His Chest

A man loves nothing better than being praised. Don't blow smoke up his tail. Just parrot back something positive that he's been twittering away about during the course of your conversation.

Love Scripts
For the man who is trying to impress you with his mental heft:
   "You're so smart. I love a man with a big brain."
   "What inspired you to study particle physics?"
   "Tell me, George, what can I do about global warming?"

For the wild man artist:

"You're so intriguing. Tell me more about [whatever he's whipping up in the studio]. I'm fascinated."

For the blue-collar, macho regular Joe:

"I am so sick of wimpy guys!"

"Ooh, can you help? The top is stuck on this ketchup bottle."

For the single, divorced father who has fought to retain custody of his kids:

"You have such a great values system."

"How is his soccer team doing this year?"

For the A-type success monger who has rattled off a long list of his accomplishments:

"What an alpha male!"

"I find you sooooo inspiring."

For the guy who's nervous and shy:

"I feel wonderful right now. It's so nice being here with you."

For the grad student who's working two jobs, too:

"What commitment and stamina. I love that kind of drive in a man! You must be an animal in the bedroom!"

For the man who is flashing his cash:

"I feel so taken care of tonight. What a treat. Thank you."

For the man who's trying to seduce you:

"I feel so sexy around you."

"You make me want to do terrible things!"

"Purrrr."

Don't do this: I was once on a date with a man, and said, "You dress like a dad."

"Well, I am a dad," he said.

"Yes," I replied, "but you're not *my* dad!"

ROMANTIC RULE: *Always remember to thank your date for dinner. (You didn't need to be reminded of that, right? Just checking.)*

How to Predict His Lovemaking Style over Dinner

Observe his body language.

- If he touches you often, he's the **reassuring** type.

- If you touches you too much, he's the **invasive** type.

- If he places his hand on the small of your back, he's a **caretaker**.

- If he's nervous and flighty, he's **nervous and flighty**.

- If his shoulders are hunched in a protective defensive stance, he's **innaccessible**.

- If his body is open and relaxed, he's **inviting**.

- If he sprawls, he's **confident**.

- If he holds his limbs in a controlled way, he's **intense**.

- If he takes your hand, or kisses it, he's romantic and **tender**.

- If he takes confident control of the waiter while ordering for you, he's **sexy!**

- If he makes sudden romantic gestures, like removing your stiletto and massaging your foot under the table, he's **working you!**

eleven

Date Interrogation

Men are like sweaters. Once you remove the tags,

they're so much harder to return.

–Lauren Frances, Ph. DD

Beware the Goose Who Lays
the Golden Egg
(aka The Secret Male Lemon Law Disclaimer)

There's a well-kept secret about men that you may not know, but once you do, it's guaranteed to save you more heartache than a six-barrel shotgun.

MAN FACT: *Men will tell you almost anything on the first two dates and then clam up for the next two years.*

After that, it will take a team of wild horses to drag him to therapy to talk about his "relationship issues." *(And aren't we just sick of that?)* That's why the best time to get information out of a man is right at the beginning of your courtship. If you listen carefully, men tell you everything you need to know about them, including whether they're worthy of you. So al-

63

ways take this golden opportunity to learn the inner secrets of your new feathered friend.

Now, men have an innate sense of honor, but they aren't stupid. No one knows their faults better than they do, so they've devised an ingenious strategy to facilitate the propagation of the species and maintain their personal integrity, *no matter what kind of sociopaths they are.*

MAN FACT: *While men are strutting their stuff, they'll also lay a golden egg.*

It'll whip right by you if you're not listening for it, but if you are, it'll surely come. While he prattles on about his stock portfolio or boasts of his world travels, your date will let slip *exactly* what's wrong with him in the relationship area.

The Secret Disclaimer is always hidden in the fine print. It will be only a sentence or two, or even a little monologue if you're lucky. But once he lets it slip, he'll camouflage it under such a magnificent display of fine feathers you'll have a hard time spotting the 666 branded right in the middle of his beautiful chest.

MAN FACT: *The Secret Male Lemon Law Disclaimer is often passed off as a joke.*

Because it's so tiny in comparison with all of his male posturing, the disclaimer may seem totally inconsequential at the time. Besides, no woman in her right mind would be so flagrantly off-putting if she actually liked someone!

> *"I'm a pervert," says he.*
> *"How funny!" thinks she.*

She'll usually dismiss it entirely, until three years later, when she sits bolt upright in the middle of the night and finally puts it all together. *He told her on their first date that he was cheating on his mistress!* She laughed right along with him at the time because she thought it was a joke, and now he's having sex with the dog walker.

LEMON LAW MAN FACT: *These gems of invaluable information often make sense only in hindsight, after three months, or three years, of wasted time and effort.*

And to top it all off, he'll think that he was a good guy for warning you about his foibles. And if you bitch about it to him later, he'll remind you that he told you from date one that he was still sleeping with his ex or that he's a powdered-doughnut freak. You see, once a man lays the golden egg, he's no longer responsible for it. *You are.* When you get hurt, it's *your* problem, because he straight up let you know, and you went right ahead and got involved with him anyway. You silently agreed to his terms; now he gets off scot-free and guilt-free, too.

Actual Lemon Law Disclaimers I've Heard on First Dates

"Why get married? You just lose half your shit!"

"People think I'm terrible for not being married, but at least I'm not cheating on my wife."

"I've never been in love."

"I only have time to date once or twice a month."

"My fiancée cheated on me with a twenty-two-year-old. I have a very short fuse now."

"My wife said she doesn't love me anymore. Why doesn't she love me?"

"The last girl I dated was eighteen."

"My ex-wife hates me."

"My ex-girlfriend was crazy! I've been single ever since."

"My longest relationship was seven months."

Seven months?! Even I couldn't pretend I hadn't heard that.

Amazingly, these lemons were all slipped into conversations during romantic dinners, in fabulous restaurants, while my dates collectively managed to boast about a $7 million home on Malibu beachfront property, legendary fame, 21 Emmys, a star on Hollywood Boulevard, 15 gold records, a cock just shy of Tommy Lee's, 350 avocado trees, tennis courts, an IQ of 156, a bankroll north of 100 mill.

They also offered to take me to Paris *(merci)*, Italy, Spain *(olé)*, Scotland (did accept this offer), London (this one, too), the Spa (yup), Turkey, Amsterdam (should have gone), Ojai (uh-huh), Vegas (pending), Puerto Vallarta (had fun!), the Caribbean . . .

All right, I'm a sucker for a fabulous trip.

One promised to give me the most fabulous orgasms on earth (true) . . . and on and on.

But remember the lemons? They make even the sweetest moments a little sour, the hottest guys become unattractive, and the richest men seem like paupers.

MAN FACT: *Now nobody's perfect, but some men are definitely more perfect than others.*

So don't kill the goose who lays the golden egg . . . thank him for it. He just saved you a lot of time and aggravation. Learn the secrets of the men who would be king of your emotional castle by carefully listening to them, and *believing* them.

ROMANTIC RULE: *Everyone has problems. You need someone who has problems you can live with.*

Mandatory Homework After Your First Date

Hop into bed, and pull out the Lovebirds' Field Notes (see page 77), and fill in your new specimen's profile without delay. Make sure to record any Lemon Law findings. If you're ridiculously attracted to him or impressed with his fine feathers, always share his Secret Male Lemon Law Disclaimer with a trusted member of your Mantrap Pack. That way, if you wind up slipping into a sex coma, your pal can give you some perspective on your fledgling romance *(he's a professional poker player, you nitwit!)*. This will help keep you abreast of your findings, and keep your head out of the clouds and your feet on the ground.

Make Him Sing Like a Canary

Some men are cagier than others. The harder it is to get a confession out of your subject, the more he usually has to tell. If your bird doesn't open up easily, you'll want to *make* him reveal his secret past by slipping him some truth serum while you're having drinks. To make him sing like a canary, ask the ultimate Heartache Prevention Question: "So, Clark, why aren't you married yet?"

Asking the Heartache Prevention Question in an off-handed way will make any man talk a blue streak, so pay very close attention to his response.

MAN FACT: *This is like putting a turban on your head, and more effective than calling the psychic network, because you'll get a little preview about how he'll talk about the both of you right after you break up!*

This is the one and only time you can ask such a loaded question without it being "heavy" because you can't possibly take the answer to this question personally . . . yet. You'll be amazed to discover how men flap their jaws with ease about deep emotional problems on a first date with total strangers. And for the women who've only been privy to this type of soul-bearing honesty from men during tearful breakups, I promise that you will be stunned.

When you ask the Heartache Prevention Question, men will tell you exactly how they feel about marriage, often revealing whether they're financially stable, are adamantly or morally opposed to the state of matrimony itself, or are having too much fun playing the field to even *think* about settling down. They'll also divulge the status of prior marriages and custody arrangements and stupidly confess about their current roster of out-of-town girlfriends as well. I am *so* not kidding.

Tip: Listen very carefully to how he talks about his exes and be on the lookout for any pet "relationship theories." He might tell you, for example, that "love doesn't really exist" or that all of his relationships "end up the same way . . . 'in court.'"

Congratulations! You have thoroughly broken your subject. He has just revealed his inner "romantic guidance system." It's what he believes to be true about relationships and love, *and it isn't going to change.* Most people just repeat their mating patterns over and over again with somebody new, and that could mean you. If he's given you troubling information, it will steer all of his relationships in the same direction . . . south. This is hard to reprogram without divine intervention — or intense therapy. Or a hard smack on the noggin.

So when he starts talking, listen up. You've hit the jackpot. The last time I administered verbal truth serum, my date leaned in and said: "I told you my ex just moved to Dallas with my seven-year-old son, didn't I? She's totally psycho!"

"No," I purred, "what happened?" I found out he'd skipped out on child support payments. I became very sleepy and called it a night.

MAN FACT: *If he says he wants to get married, but that all of his exes are stalkers, he's just a Bat Out of Hell in a Penguin suit.*

When you hear information like this, *believe him.* The next question to ask is "*Have you gone to therapy for that?*"

If he says yes, ask him if it's *working.*

So If It Walks Like a Duck . . .

Q: *If a man reveals that he was chronically unfaithful to his wife, went to prison for assault, and has vowed to never remarry . . .*

A: He is an unfaithful, violent, and very hardened bachelor.

MAN FACT: *If it walks like a duck and talks like a duck . . . he's a dick!*

You are now dating like an international spy.

If you've followed my instructions thus far, you'll have thoroughly be-witched your Lovebird, and he'll have revealed his innermost secrets to you. He'll feel so connected to you that he'll have lowered his guard, dropped the drawbridge, and invited you right into the castle of his inner self.

The tiny questions you ask, the way you mirror his body move-ments, the attention and validation you give him — these will be like a narcotic to him. Your date will have become very open, intimate, and even, gasp, *vulnerable.*

But heed this warning: Don't get too comfortable and jump right in and start telling your war stories, too, or your entire evening will turn into a therapy session.

ROMANTIC RULE: *Don't become his therapist! When your subject opens up, actively listen.*

Nod your head sympathetically and say:

"Ahhhh."

"Hmmm . . . I get it."

"Wow, you must be strong to have survived that."

"That must have been soooo difficult."

"You seem so well adjusted. Did you go to therapy for that?"

"Waiter, check please!

Then go home, strip off your gloves, and hop right into the tub. Congratulations on a job well done!

twelve

Clay Pigeons

In truth, you don't need a million men, just a fun flock of runners-up, until a true Lovebird comes in for a landing. Sadly, there's no way to play the field without incurring dating disappointments and some downright failures. This fact won't be quite as daunting once you learn how to swiftly terminate a failed romantic experiment. This chapter gives you all the ammo you need to shoot the lame ducks down.

How to Handle Turbulence

You're both having a great time, when *bam,* all of a sudden you hit a bad patch and you find yourself gripping your seat.

Don't panic.

Turbulence is always a cue to excuse yourself and retire to the powder room. Get a breath of fresh air and slowly reapply your lip gloss. After a little touch-up, you may come back completely refreshed and find that your date's ruffled feathers have smoothed down, too. But if turbulence continues for more than several minutes (five), simply part ways. You're in for a very bumpy ride, so just deplane.

ROMANTIC RULE: *Don't bother trying to work things out if you hit an extended rough patch too soon.*

TRUE STORY: Once, while on a terrible date, my aunt Pat excused herself from the table, slipped the waiter a $10 bill, and said, "Tell the man in the corner booth that I'm leaving and that I'm never coming back!"

Don't you love that?

Terrible Turbulence
Always Shoot a Man Down If:

- He has the nerve to check out other women in front of you.

- He's too sexually forward.

- You're bored out of your mind.

- He insults you.

- He out and out flirts with another woman!

- He's disrespectful.

- He's in a bad mood.

- He starts a fight.

Tell these Turkeys to buzz off and quickly hail yourself a cab!

ROMANTIC RULE: *Never get into a car with a man whom you barely know if he begins fighting with you or is in a terrible mood.*

"Was He Winging It?"

When a man . . .

- wants to meet for a drink after his workout because he's "already eaten," **he's cheap.**

- asks you in a whiny voice, "What would you like to do?" and has nothing fun to suggest, he's a **lazy whiner.**

- makes out with you, vanishes, and reappears several days later, he's a **booty-call.**

- wants you to meet him somewhere very low-key, **he's married.**

- takes you to the mall or a fast-food restaurant and says he's keeping the date "real," **he's broke.**

- spends money on you and takes you to special places, and then stops doing it, he's sending you a message: **You're demoted.**

- doesn't put any thought or effort into figuring out how to spend quality time with you, aka not investing in your relationship, he's a **nitwit.**

- only expends an effort of the sexual kind, **he's not your husband!**

Shoot 'Em Down
with the Dear John Phoner

The face-to-face breakup is overrated and only necessary if you were dating each other for some time. When you need to cut a man loose, end the date as soon as humanly possible and extend your right hand for a quick little shake. Period. If he calls and tries to bore you to tears again, simply break the bad news to him over the telephone.

MAN FACT: *Being rejected over the phone is far less humiliating to a man than being shot down at close range because it allows him to save face.*

Instead, knock him off his perch, hang up, and allow him to lick his wounds in private. The Dear John Phoner also protects you from any angry outbursts of temper and has other added benefits: no awkward partings, uncomfortable car rides, or indigestion after dining.

Love Script for the Dear John Phoner
Simply say in a pleasant but decisive way, **"After thinking about it, I just don't feel we're a match. Sorry, Charlie."**

If he asks the dreaded **"Why?"** simply state, **"It's just my gut feeling. It's just not clicking for me. I'm sorry. Take care now,"** and then get right off the phone.

Always remember: No one can ever argue with a gut feeling. It's invulnerable to attack. Even in Milan.

Irritating and Intrusive Birdcalls

"No" is a complete sentence. If a man repeatedly calls after you've told him that you don't want to see him, screen his calls and don't ever return them again. You have set a boundary, and the boundary is NO. If you allow him to bully or wheedle his way back in, you'll have no one but yourself to blame. If you shut the little pecker out, he'll eventually tire of this game and move on.

ROMANTIC RULE: *You must learn how to say no if you want to say yes to the right man. All the rest are just romantic detours!*

Is He Bowing Out?

If he doesn't compliment you . . .

If he doesn't walk you to your door . . .

If he doesn't say he had a great time . . .

If he doesn't try to touch you . . .

If he doesn't talk about future plans . . .

If he says, "I'll call you," without any enthusiasm . . .

If he doesn't try to kiss you good-bye . . .

If he peels out before you're inside your front door . . .

. . . he's bowing out.

He was just a Clay Pigeon. Write him off as failed research. Don't bother wasting your time trying to figure out why he doesn't want to pursue you. You can never accurately figure out why things don't click with men whom you barely know.

I subscribe to the old adage "Their rejection is God's protection." If you have to make up a story about why he's bowing out, it's always better to make up one that makes you feel better, instead of one designed for self-torture! This kind of date replay can make a woman want to hide under her covers and give up on men altogether if it's indulged in too often. It's a very bad habit to persist in, and even worse than nail biting.

Instead, why not try this on for size? He was terribly attracted to you but suspected you'd have a zero-tolerance policy about his erectile dysfunction. Better, right?

I knew the truth would set you free!

ROMANTIC RULE: *Don't turn the gun on yourself! Always shoot down Clay Pigeons.*

thirteen

Lovebirds' Field Notes Checklist

Was He Winging It?

Your Lovebirds' Field Notes

It is essential to take thorough field notes of your romantic research. Use the handy checklist below to identify and catalog the different types of birds that you've lured to your side. If you've been observant, you'll have gleaned important clues about which members of your flock are serious contenders for mating purposes, just naughty playthings, or birds to set free immediately!

Basic Info

Bird name

Telephone number

E-mail address

Species

Subspecies

Date Assessment

Arrival time

Location of date

Did he make reservations?

Do you have any reservations about him?

Conversational skills

Courtesy level

Date attentiveness

Was he cheap?

What did he invest: attention, $, or enthusiasm?

Birdsong and compliments

Departure information

Good-night kiss

Did he try to rebook you?

Did you have fun?

Bored to tears

On cloud 9

Smooth sailing

Turbulence

Entertaining

Would have rather done laundry

Temperament

Cooing Dove

Wounded Bird

Peckish and Irritable

Confident Cock of the Walk

Aggressive Condor

Predatory Raptor

Ruffled feathers

Too withdrawn, hunched, drooping wings

Flighty and nervous

Settled and relaxed

Narcissistic Peacock

Cockfighting Peckerhead

Grooming

Neat and clean

Rumpled

Messy

Condition of teeth

Errant hairs

Warts

Hair gel

Body odor

Halitosis

Gas

Cheap cologne

Your Attraction Level (Rate on a scale of 1 to 5)

His physique

His big brain

His wallet _____

His lifestyle _____

His sense of humor _____

His care of you _____

His spirituality _____

His creativity _____

His values system _____

Sexual chemistry _____

Your pheromone attraction level _____

His Maserati _____

Flying in the same direction _____

Character Assessment

Is he employed? _____

Red flags _____

Secret Male Lemon Law Disclaimer _____

Unusual traits or habits _____

Is he unresolved about any past relationships? _____

Is he on good terms with his family, his coworkers, his ex-wives or girlfriends?

Would you leave a child in his care? _____

Are there any causes he is committed to? _____

Does he do charity work? _____

Is he spiritually inclined? _____

Is he a member of a spiritual community, or charity?

Do you have friends in common?

How did he check out?

Does he have pets?

Any plants?

Life Stage

How old is this bird?

What are his relationship goals?

What are his personal goals?

Is he a parent, or a big brother?

How involved is he with their care?

Does he own his own home or condo?

Does he have investments (planning for his future)?

Does he feel like a success in the workplace?

Life stage of your bird (Juvenile, Breeding, or Nesting)

Is He Socialized?

Does he display any aggressive behavior?

Road rage, sharp tongue, rudeness to you or others?

Is he insulting in any way?

Was he too sexually aggressive?

Did he put you on the defensive?

Did he check out other women?

Did he try to make you jealous?

Does he have commitment issues or poor relationship history?

Vocalizing Skills and Conversational Style

Flowing

Seems bored

Sparkling

Snappy

Fun

Attentive

Engaged

Like pulling teeth

Sense of Humor

This often indicates his IQ level and nagging insecurities.

Witty

Smart

Dry

Sarcastic

Funny

Childish

Sexual banter

Downright dirty

Mean-spirited

At another's expense

At your expense

Nonexistent

Compatibility Cues

Is he an early bird or a night owl?

Ready for nesting

Predatory Raptor

Juvenile male

Snowy Owl

Was he a Lame Duck?

Is he a fledgling (too young, or unemployed)?

Does he have an attitude problem?

Does he love his mother?

Does he love her too much?

Is he flying right?

Compatible relationship goals

Health Check

Medical problems

Activity level

Energy level

Alcoholism

Addictions: drugs, gambling, food, sex

Workaholic: _____

ADD _____

STDs _____

Conclusions

Significant findings _____

Date assessment _____

Your comfort level _____

Your attraction level _____

Your romantic prediction _____

Drop from the flock? _____

His date rating _____

The Five-Star Date-Rating System

This five-star date-rating system for date classification purposes will help you keep on top of your flock!

- Complete interest is five stars. ★★★★★

- If you called a man and he doesn't return the call within two or three days, he absolutely loses a star.

- If he drops below three stars, he's on date probation.

- If he drops below three stars and then tries to fly back into formation and calls you out of the blue, he can earn a star back, if you so choose.

Author's Note: In the past, I've had someone down to one star, another one was star-free, and another was actually a black hole!

Now remember, not everybody starts out with five stars. If you're not really attracted to him, he can start out with only three stars and work his way up. Or screw up once and he's out. And for the record, he loses a star for hair gel and two for bad cologne.

Happy hunting!

Men and women both want to get each other
on their knees, but for very different reasons!

    −Lauren Frances, Ph. DD

mating

part ii

Shopping for men is exactly like ... shopping!

–Lauren Frances, Ph. DD

fourteen

Bird Selection

Man selection should follow the same guidelines as successful pet selection. Choose a man who possesses an even-keeled and loving temperament. He should be cooperative, reasonable, well-mannered, and easy to train. Housebroken would be nice, too. But if a man requires excessive punishment, attention, and emotional energy, it's probably unwise to keep your pet . . . I mean, man.

Go for the domesticated bird. When selecting the right male for you, it's always a boon if he's already been domesticated. Men who've been in successful long-term relationships tend to fall into this category. These men are like self-walking dogs! The upside for the already housebroken male is obvious. He'll grab some Midol for you while he's out buying beer and has mastered the difficult phrase "No problem," and the harder "Yes dear." But he'll still throw wet towels on the bed.

Always consider the predomesticated male. This man was raised by a loving single mother. Not only is he pretrained, he keeps house far better than you and knows about secret cleaning techniques *like bleaching the sink!* The downside: Your towel-folding methods may be held up to ridicule. The predomesticated male makes for an incredibly well-trained and sensitive partner, unless he has "issues" with Mom. Then he's virtually untamable and is probably better left outdoors.

The garden-variety wild birdman. Unwilling to modify his behavior for the indoors, the wild birdman lives under the radar and flies above the law — Female Law, that is — as in socks in the hamper and no tequila after dawn. He rips through your house like a tornado. He gets miffed if he feels he's been criticized. Helpful comments like "You should've made a left at that stop sign, babe" can make this sensitive bird fly into a snit! Many women agree that the wild birdman is the most common species of male around. Once you learn how to manhandle him, however (see Part Three), you may discover he makes quite a delightful partner.

Beware the previously owned problem bird. Sometimes even the most adorable man exhibits antisocial behavior after a small "settling in" period. He suddenly becomes cocky, rude, and uncooperative or, worse, he transforms into a world-class screamer or nitpicking fussbudget. This change in temperament occurs the second he thinks he's got his talons wrapped right around your little finger. In order for him to be a tolerable housemate, you'll need to take this bird down a notch or two and give him an Altitude Adjustment. (*See* Give Him an Altitude Adjustment, page 191.)
The Upside: You get to wear leather gloves in the bedroom.

Predatory Raptors

Once upon a time there was a very bored but beautiful princess. Then one day, her hero came charging in....

You hyperventilate as he artfully kisses you, bites your neck, and tells you everything he already knows that you want to hear. He will make you his, and his alone. He's hell-bent on it. This usually won't take very long, maybe only a couple of weeks of intense phone-calling, two-waying, and sweet-talking.

But once you get hooked on his attention, he suddenly disappears, leaving you all alone in your (now) drafty turret, peering out of tiny windows and wondering where he went. You fervently pray for his speedy return; in distress, you consult the court's fortune-tellers for answers.

"What happened? Did I say something wrong? Did I hurt his feelings?" you ask your girlfriends in a panic.

Of course you didn't! He just knew how to work you into a state of intense *romantic hopefulness.*

You're shocked when you figure out what was behind the big hard-on he used to knock you off balance with. He was just jousting! You didn't realize he was in this for sport, and are stunned to find that you were put on a pedestal only to be knocked on your ass.

Still, you can't stop thinking about him, or talking about him, and wondering where he went. And when he's coming back. You feel a little crazy. You're now plagued with positively torturous medieval longing.

The Queen noticed that Lancelot avoided her now and rode away from Camelot on every quest that was offered. She sent for him and said: "Lance, I see and feel daily that your love for me grows less, and you ride ever to help damsels in distress. Have you perhaps found one who is dearer to your heart than I?"

You'll have to wait more than a little while for Lance-a-lots to return. These types of men are busy. So many women to bone, so little time! Maybe that's why he was in such a rush after all.

Then, miraculously, he calls (*see* Wild Blue Yonder Caller, page

159). You're elated! He gives you some lame excuse about why he couldn't call you: *"An infestation of rats overran the castle." "A bunch of us feudal lords went on a snowboarding trip. The powder was perfect."*

You accept his lack of apology immediately because he has managed to make you feel *really* insecure. You didn't like being tossed aside and want to be lovingly placed back where you know you deserve to be. If not up on a pedestal, then any old chair will do. Oh, who are we kidding; you'll be on your knees the next time you see him!

Q: What happened?

A: By building up your expectations and then dashing them just as fast, the Predatory Raptor knocks you off center and now has the upper hand. This is a manipulation, and he knows it. BE-WARE!! The Predatory Raptor is no Lovebird, my lady. If he were, he wouldn't have loved you and left you holding the emotional bag.

MAN FACT: *If you're spending a lot of time wondering what's happening, he's probably wandering!*

Lesson: We don't want men we have to contact on the astral plane. We want men we can actually talk to and who show up on Friday night to take us out for sushi.

ROMANTIC RULE: *Be suspicious of men who try to rush into (or out of) anything too soon, like a storybook romance and your pantaloons.*

The Wounded Bird
(aka the Instant Boyfriend)

The Instant Boyfriend starts out being quite charming . . . for two or three dates. Then he'll try to control you with displays of immediate and intense possessiveness. Setting up expectations of future Us-ness, he begins his onslaught by calling you every day, sometimes multiple times a day. *Problem:* You've only been dating one week! He's actually doing this surveillance to keep tabs on you and to create a No-Fly Zone for other incoming males. This is a passive way of locking you in his little tower, and the telephone is his wrought iron key.

The Wounded Bird has "Broken Wing Syndrome." This display of (faux) vulnerability is actually a powerful technique he uses to ex-cuse his suspicious and needy behavior.

Translation: I was cheated on by my last girlfriend so I'm going to drive you crazy by crowding you and checking up on you in ways that you can't even imagine.

The Wounded Bird is manipulative. Instant Boyfriends also some-times turn into instant stalkers. What starts out as "cute" often be-comes oppressive, smothering, and controlling.

Case Study: The Wounded Bird
Louise, 31, model/waitress
Frank, 42, therapist

I met Frank at work. He was cute so I gave him my number. He im-mediately started calling every day and wanting to speak every night. He said his ex-wife cheated on him with a twenty-two-year-old. He still seemed really angry about it. We had only gone on three dates when he started saying things like "Do you miss me?" I wasn't quite sure how to respond, so I played along.

One night, I didn't return a message he'd left. I was tired, and after all, we'd only been dating for a week and a half! He wasn't really my boyfriend yet. He gave me a very hard time about it, grilling me about why I didn't want to speak to him. I told him several times that I was just tired after a long night's work. Just talking to him started feeling like a lot of work!

In the beginning, he seemed so interested in my life, unlike a lot of other guys. He would ask questions in such a nice way that I'd tell him everything.

"So what did you do today, where were you? Did you have fun? Who were you hanging out with? Were there any guys there? Did you talk to any of them?" That's when I realized he was actually quizzing me to keep tabs on me! I told him I wanted to stop seeing him, and he got very angry about it. *Dating this man felt like joining a cult.* I finally stopped taking his calls, but it took him awhile to get the message.

Lesson: If you're feeling smothered or controlled as quickly as all that, drop him in two seconds flat.

Marrying Men and Bachelors

There are only two kinds of men in this world, marrying men and bachelors. Marrying men *like* being in relationships with women. In fact, they need them. Now, "need" isn't the dirty word we've been taught to revile, because in truth, men only marry the women they need. Otherwise, they'd just keep burning through women and replacing them with different models . . . who sometimes *are* models. Whoops! Allow me to refocus.

Marrying men prefer having a special someone to call every day. The *same* someone. These men are often categorized as serial monogamists, but this makes them sound like criminals. This is so unfair because, in truth, they are wonderful!

MAN FACT: *Men who are emotionally available show up immediately. They don't have dramatic problems that prevent them from moving a relationship forward.*

A guy prime for the plucking is direct, makes his intentions clear, and usually proposes within six months to one year. He's landed that big job, is ready to buy that house, and has finally stopped wanting to have sex with his ex. He feels good about himself, but hopefully not **too** good. Actually, it would be best if he felt a tad insecure . . . and vulnerable enough to be grateful that God sent him another chance at love . . . in the form of **you.**

Men Prime for the Plucking...

- Feel incomplete being single.

- Move from one serious relationship to the next.

- Say things like "I'm looking to get married" with the ease of a man saying, "My company is looking for a receptionist."

- Use the words *we, us,* and *when.*

- Bring up the subject of marriage, family, and commitment on their own, unflinchingly, and without prodding.

- Ask qualifying questions like *"What was your last relationship like?"* or say, *"I can't believe you're not married yet!"*

You can relax around such a man because he's taking care of business, which means you can quite happily take care of his bizness!

Cocks of the Walk
(aka the Hardened Bachelor)

And then there are bachelors. They can take women or leave them, and so often do. Because they have poor relationship skills, bachelors become masters of seduction or they'd *never* get laid.

The Hardened Bachelor has an idealized fantasy that no mortal woman can live up to, or would want to. He'll treat you like a goddess and worship at your shrine for an intoxicating three weeks to three months, but beware! He'll become strangely repulsed by your allergy to dust and get turned off when he discovers that you're *human*.

If you think these men have hearts of stone, though, you're wrong. The Hardened Bachelor is *deeply* in love . . . with himself. Note: This man is selfish except when it comes to sex. And that's where you come in. Right through the little zippered door!

ROMANTIC RULE: *The bachelor needs only one thing from women: sex. And he gets this for free from most women without any kind of commitment at all, maybe just for the price of one dinner!*

The Hardened Bachelor has unreasonable needs for "space" that no woman can withstand and are meant to drive her away. His rigid boundaries ensure that you'll remain too distant for real intimacy/expectation to occur. As soon as he feels he's being emotionally hemmed in, he *panics*. This is one reason why this type of man prefers dating very young women. He knows that most girls aren't ready for marriage and won't pressure him in any way that he can't easily handle. Besides, young girls look fantastic in a thong and just want to party! And so, I might add, does he.

MAN FACT: *Hardened Bachelors feel that women are to be used for their pleasure and then replaced, kind of like batteries. Are you disposable? I don't think so!*

Identifying Characteristics of the Hardened Bachelor

- Is still traumatized from a twisted relationship deep in his past — with Mommy or an ex — that even therapy can't undo.

- Makes wisecracks about how "unhappy" all of his happily married friends are.

- Uses the words *me, mine,* and *maybe.*

- If he *was* married, he definitely cheated!

- Goes through women like truckers guzzling coffee at a rest stop.

A Hardened Bachelor Only
Marries When . . .

A. He "accidentally" knocks up a twenty-two-year-old (she plans this) and then he'll try to do the right thing. But he'll hate family life, cheat on her, blame her for it, leave her, and then bitch about it for the next seventeen years.

B. Some life-changing event occurs and he has a total change of relationship perspective. This could look like turning fifty, having a near-death experience (ball cancer), or erectile dysfunction. His lifestyle now seems a tad shallow and self-centered, even to him, and he suddenly longs for, dare I say it, family life. So he sets about procuring a young wife who'll look hot in a nurse's uniform while pushing his wheelchair in his golden years.

C. He runs across a woman who has such incredible self-esteem that she refuses to sell herself out. She sets a standard that he'll need to rise to if he wants to bed her (*see* Annette Bening). This will stun him, irritate him, and titillate him into evolving into a better man, but this kind of transformation is so rare that it's almost not worth mentioning.

BEWARE : If a Hardened Bachelor actually lets his guard down long enough to fall in love with you, he'll be virtually tool-free when it comes to working on a real relationship. He's often immature, petty, and prone to terrible fits of jealousy, and he comes with a slew of totally dysfunctional behaviors. You'll soon discover that the only thing that he's learned to work out with a woman is located in his BVDs.

The Dominant Cocks of the Walk
(aka George Clooney Syndrome)

He's in his forties and is still so fine that he feels no pressure to settle down. The ladies love him, his career is on fire, and there is no end of T&A in sight. He can date in every age range and bed whomever he wants because he's charismatic, handsome, and, well, . . . him. He's a master at making women feel really, really special because he *loves* them. One at a time, or in delightful combinations of twos and threes!

These men aren't monogamous. They don't have to be. Besides, what's a bonbon or two when you've been offered the whole damn box?

Men with George Clooney Syndrome fly in tight flocks composed of other rich, sexy, and equally unavailable males. Their long-term primary relationships are often with one another. But they *are* available to women for sex and fun, or long-term, nonexclusive sexual arrangements, and sometimes high-profile marriages riddled with extramarital liaisons.

Unless you're a soaring starlet, you'll find this man impossible to nest with. These guys won't slow down or become eligible for marriage until they hit their mid to late fifties, and by then, who wants 'em?

WARNING: These swinging bachelors are perfect for awesome rocking chair memories. It's thrilling to be with them, but you may get a little dizzy from the intense ups and downs. So take it lying down! Enjoy the ride, but don't say I didn't warn you when it comes to its abrupt, inevitable, and heart-wrenching end.

Yeah, I know . . . that's why God made girlfriends.

fifteen

Don't Count Your Chickens Before They Hatch!

The Heartache Prevention Handbook

Girls love to jump to romantic conclusions. This phenomenon usually starts occurring in junior high, when they write a boy's name all over their biology homework with small hearts over the i's. Here's a page of my own seventh-grade handiwork:

David Boyd
D. Boyd
Mrs. David Boyd.
Mr. and Mrs. David & Lauren Boyd
Lauren Boyd . . .
mmmmmmmmmmm

All right. I never even kissed David Boyd. But I did spend many a dreamy hour in seventh grade very much married to him . . . *in my mind.* If David Boyd had known that I actually liked him (and to what an extent!) he would've been shocked. I managed to conceal my love for him entirely. I worshipped him in the private way of a thirteen-year-old girl who'd find romantic exposure almost as mortifying as wearing a two-piece bathing suit to the community swim club.

Years later, I learned the downside of emotionally jumping the gun: Men don't like it! It makes them feel pressured and uptight. And peevishly accuse you of being *needy*.

Jumping to romantic conclusions* about a fledgling romance is always dangerous because you run the risk of accidentally improving the story you wrote (either all by yourself, or with the help of excitable girlfriends) while you're out on a third date. It'll make most men want to bolt out your door, right after they feel you up.

Scientific Fact: You can't remove the observer from the experiment. When you become too smitten with your subject, you run the risk of losing your keen powers of observation.

If you count your chickens before they hatch, you'll also miss important cues screaming, *"Danger! Abort mission!"*

WARNING: Men will initially be on their best behavior to try to convince you that they're the great guys they've smartly deduced you *need* them to be . . . after all, it's so much easier to get laid that way!

Now to be fair, even the most seasoned Romantic Researcher will be tempted to forget her basic training and act like a total teenager (novice) in the field, when being courted by a hot-ass man. She may make silly manhandling mistakes (like confessing how long she's been sex-free) and wind up butt-naked in a Hummer. So stay alert: Don't contaminate your romantic research by throwing caution** to the wind.

Solution: Slow down! There are HUGE gaps of Intel missing. Trust is created over the course of time, when a man's *actions* also match his *words*. To protect yourself from unnecessary dating disappointment, call up a trusted member of your Mantrap Pack and run your romantic findings by her. Getting a second opinion will ensure

---

* Romantic projection
** Your panties

that you keep following good manhandling protocol, and prevent you from getting so looped that you can't see the forest for the trees, and the birds from the bees.

ROMANTIC RULE: *If you're on page 126 of* Love Story *and he's just flipping through* Penthouse, *your romance may be Much Ado About Nothing.*

Or break out the karma sutra and get on the same page . . . *together!*

Stop Filling in the Blanks

You both love Victorian novels, having sex in broom closets, and eating key lime pies. You think, *Mon Dieu!* this man is perfect for me!
Or is he?

WARNING: Faulty romantic research will make excitable women jump to inaccurate conclusions.

Example: Your date arrives right on time, and you ask him to have a seat on the couch while you decide which handbag to use. As you slink back into the living room, you observe him trying to play with your *very* unfriendly cat . . .

Dot 1: "Oh, look at kitty," you think to yourself. "He really likes the New Guy! . . . Uh-oh . . . kitty's trying to crawl up New Guy's shirt and sit on his head. OUCH! That must've hurt, but he's not even getting mad. Wow, what a good sport!"

Dot 2: "I love him!"

Dot 3: "He's going be an amazing dad!"

Now, I, ask you, how did you get from dot one to dot three? Uh-oh. You connected another dot . . . while we were talking!

Dot 4: "We'd have gorgeous kids!"

And another . . .

Dot 5: "He would look so adorable coaching Little League!"

You just connected the dots and drew the picture that you wanted to see! See?

And now you quickly start to color it in. What you don't know is that Howard recently had a vasectomy. When he blurts it out six months from now, you'll let it go right by: "Well, it's reversible! I'm sure he'll get his plumbing fixed once we're engaged!"

Problem: You fail to have this conversation with him now. Oh, you'll have the talk all right, *two years* from now. And girl, you are gonna be *pissed!*

In the meantime, you'll want to believe that what you hope to be true . . . will be.

Faulty Romantic Towers

Commonly referred to as "building castles in the air," Romantic Faulty Towers are constructed through a combination of romantic wish fulfillment and willful denial. Instead of connecting the dots and seeing a skull and crossbones staring back at you, you'll cleverly move the dots around and make a picture that's more to your liking.

"Hey, if I erase dot thirty-two and just move it over here, that skull and crossbones actually looks like . . . a crown! I love crowns!"

We have now reached the end of objectivity and sanity. Your friends shake their heads collectively and say, "What on earth do you see in him? He's a skirt chaser, a gambler, a goofball, a nitwit! We just don't get it!" but you'll be completely incapable of seeing it. You fell in love with the pretty picture you drew and won't take it off the fridge.

ROMANTIC RULE: *When you stop seeing what's happening (denial) and you start making up your own story, you'll usually start to believe it!*

WARNING: Connecting the dots and drawing your own picture will blur your romantic vision. **Wishful Thinking** is a terrible time-wasting trap. It'll cause you to fall for men whose goals are completely at odds with yours, and pretend that they'll magically transform *all by themselves* into the men of your dreams someday. Unfortunately, that day is so not right now! This is also called Romance Novel Writing 101.*

When women connect the dots, they cannot correctly (or quickly) assess their suitors. This lack of discernment will cause them to fall for unsuitable characters, and mistakenly reject men of real value.

The upside: Not being able to spot Mr. Wrong soon enough is a terrible waste of a girl's time, but often an excellent use of her lingerie!

If this sounds like you, don't despair. You just need to get a little dating technology under your garter belt. (Or black belt.)

---

* Feel free to send your fantasy writing to my Web site, laurenfrances.net!

MANDATORY HOMEWORK: If you just started dating a "special someone" last week and think he might be *the One*, ask yourself the following questions:

1. Have you had this feeling before?
2. How many times? (Did I hear you say twelve?)
3. Are you basing your current feelings on intuition, or absolute *certainty?*

If your intuition is accurate 100 percent of the time, call me. I've lost an earring and I can't find it anywhere! For the rest of you who are positive your plane's going to crash (but it doesn't), are sure you'll never fall in love again (and you do), or find tarantulas in the bathtub that turn out to be garden spiders, you need to fact-check your intuition against the red pen of time itself because it'll take months before you figure out exactly who you're swapping spit with.

Q: Why did God make stilettos?

A: So a woman would watch her step while being courted, and walk through, not run right past, the courtship phase of her romance!

That's a fact.

Mistaking Chemistry for Compatibility

Even the most no-nonsense woman can be swept off her feet by intense arousal, confusing physical chemistry with emotional compatibility.

COMPATIBILITY *n* 1. a feeling of sympathetic understanding 2. You both love to-furkey and dream of living in a hemp village in Tucson.

ROMANTIC RULE: *Sexual chemistry proves that you're compatible in one room . . . the bedroom!*

You need to get along in the living room, the kitchen, and dining room, too. So let's snap you out of your sex coma and find out where your relationship is really headed. And put your pants back on. They're right over there. Under the sofa. Thank you.

How Compatible Are You?

Every relationship has day-to-day conflicts. These can be smoothed out by tolerance, patience, and mutual loving-kindness. Conflicting agendas and habits, however, turn even the most epic lovers into sparring partners.

When partners have different plans for their relationship's destination, it's inevitable that they won't keep happily winging away for any extended period of time. They'll either drift apart, fight for control, or get their needs hijacked by the other. That's why it's imperative to check for compatibility *outside* of the bedroom before hopping on-board.

ROMANTIC RULE: *When partners have different agendas, it's inevitable that their conflicting needs will disrupt their long term happiness.*

The Compatibility Coordinates Checklist

Always make sure to interrogate men thoroughly before choosing to give them the gift of your exclusivity. The answers to these questions will reveal whether they're really worth it!

	YES	NO
Do you have the same relationship goals? (Marriage, open relationship, exclusive relationship without marriage?)	___	___
Do you have compatible religious beliefs?	___	___
Do you both want to have children?	___	___
Do you want to live in the same location?	___	___
Do you want the same kind of lifestyle?	___	___
Do you have similar habits? (Smoking, drinking, vegetarian)	___	___
Do you or your partner have a habit or compulsion or secret that could undermine the well-being and trust of the other person? (Active addiction, penchant for cheating, criminal record)	___	___
Do you have the same values system?	___	___
Do you agree on how to handle your finances — joint or otherwise?	___	___
Do you have deal breakers that would prevent your relationship from culminating in the fulfillment of your relationship goals?	___	___

ROMANTIC RULE: *Knowledge is power, so glean important informa-tion about your real compatibility with men as soon as possible. Don't mistake a Vulture for a Robin Redbreast ever again!*

The Velvet Hammer:
The Art of Invisible Interrogation

The best way to extract this information is to slip qualifying ques-tions into conversation. Talking in a casual way won't alarm him, and he'll chime in quite naturally as a matter of course. An overt interrogation is never advisable (unless you're hammering out the terms of your relationship . . . which makes it a *conversation*, not an interrogation). Always remember to bring up topics that would be deal breakers for you. Cover only one or two of the following questions per "session."

Wondering what his plans are for the future? Try this:
"I'd love to live in the hills and swap my Boxter for a truck. Where do you see yourself living five years from now?"

Concerned about how he handles the money honey? Then toss this his way:
"I need to hire a financial planner. Do you have someone that you work with? I'd love to hear your experience with that."

MANHANDLING MANEUVER: *Bringing up hot topics in the third person will make it easier to suss him out.*

If you're curious about if he has a pre-nup on his mind:
"My coworker's fiancé hit her with a prenup the day after their engagement party . . . and she makes more than he does! She was shocked. They should've handled that discussion before the wedding invitations went out, don't you think?"

Or *"I have a friend who called off her engagement because her fiancé just told her he'd refuse to raise their children with religion in the home. And she's a Sunday school teacher! Can you believe it?"*

You get the idea. Talking about potential deal breakers in an offhanded way will allow you to discover valuable information without directly confronting or startling your birds. Having a light touch is best, and these conversations are a *must*.

Note: Unlike the three-hit rule in Battleship, one strike on this list may be enough to torpedo any romance, so find answers to these questions as soon as you're able. For the record, it's possible to survive major incompatibilities and differences as long as you both don't pretend they'll magically disappear, and you take responsibility for what you're both signing up for. You may successfully survive major incompatibilities if both partners "agree to disagree," and come up with a workable compromise. Relationship negotiation and communication always rules the roost!

(*See* James Carville and Mary Matalin.)

Homework: Get a red pen; make a list of the pros and cons of your relationship. Then make a list of all of the things you are looking for in a man, and see if the two columns match up, Buttercup!

Flush 'Em Out of the Bush!

It takes years for some women to discover that the men they are exclusive with, and completely in love with, had hidden objections about them right from the beginning; objections that have prevented them from committing fully!

Why don't men tell you the truth from the very outset instead of wasting your time?

> **The answer is simple: They don't want you to think they're bad guys. They know that breaking the news would only hurt your feelings and decrease their odds of bedding you again, so they totally fail to see the upside.**

What men don't realize is that your feelings will ultimately be hurt anyway and so much more so three years down the road! So, to save yourself a lot of time and heartache, use this brilliant manhandling maneuver that a colleague of mine invented to flush unworthy men right out of the bush.

Case Study: Flush 'Em Out of the Bush!
Andrea, 38, TV producer/writer

I hate being rejected, so I cut to the chase very quickly. In the after-glow, right after we've had fabulous sex for the first or second time, I look over and say, "Dirk, I think you're amazing, but I just don't think things could ever work out between us. I'm so bummed!"

Flabbergasted, the guy will always ask me why. Then I list all the things I fear he'll ultimately have a problem with:

I live thirty miles away.

I have a pet iguana.

I'm eight years older than you.

I'm a nudist Buddhist flutist.

I throw down the gauntlet. If he doesn't put up a fight to keep see-ing me, or worse, actually agrees with me, I know he's not "the One." We've had our fun and now I'm done.

But if he says, "I love older women! And you can practice your flute in the nude for me anytime. Or on my flute for that matter. Come on baby, I'm crazy about you, I want to keep seeing you," then I know that this man is worth my time. He's reassured me that he's comfortable with things that I could not or would not ever want to change about myself, and that he can handle my baggage. He's fought for the right to keep dating me, and to keep petting my iguana!

ROMANTIC RULE: *It's better to get thrown out of the car going ten miles per hour than sixty!*

You Can't Turn a Raven into a Dove

All men, even Pink Flamingos, live by the motto "If it ain't broke, don't fix it."

Translation: *"Don't bother trying to change our relationship, or me. Well, on second thought, maybe you can buy me shirts."*

MAN FACT: *No man ever thinks he needs fixing, and the only ones that do are on meds and think they're all better now.*

We are so screwed.

It may be hard for you to believe, but men actually *like* the way they are and have things set up exactly the way they want them when you meet them. They don't like to have you, or anyone else for that matter, pipe up and offer them helpful advice. Unless they ask for it. And even if they ask for it, they'll usually decide not to take it, and if they do, they'll pretend that it was their idea all along.

MAN FACT: *All men want to be loved exactly the way they are. They don't want to have to change for us, even if they lie and say they really, really want to. They just said that because they really, really want to have sex with you!*

The list of things he is attached to includes, but is not limited to:

Every single one of his bad habits

The leaky beanbag chair in his living room

His religion (or lack thereof)

His moronic friends

Flatulence, belching, and knuckle cracking

Negotiables: His clothing, grooming, and, god willing, back waxing. In other words, anything on his person that rubs up against you and totally grosses you out.

Non-negotiables: The big stuff. And also a bunch of the small stuff too.

Hundreds of years of research have shown that no woman, no matter how determined, can change a Raven into a Dove. It just won't work. He'll simply resist, resent, and then reject!

ROMANTIC RULE: *Never date a man's potential. It'll only drive you insane. With men, what you see really is what you get.*

Tip: When you move in together, you can throw all of his crappy stuff out and blame it on the movers.

sixteen

Flock Consciousness in the Field

"Oh just look at her, Melly! She's flirting with every man in sight."

"Don't be angry with her, India dear. Scarlett's so attractive all the men just naturally flock to her."

— Gone With the Wind

If you've been following this Man Plan, your romantic roster will be teeming with activity. You may find yourself in a new predicament: instead of being date-free, you'll become seriously overbooked! It's time to learn how to create a pecking order so you'll be able to date more than one man at a time without creating a cockfight.

Pecking Order

Here's a ground rule: Don't let men clip your wings! It's important to set boundaries with your new feathered friends. There's *no reason* to give new flock members information about the competition. Never reveal facts about your romantic roster until a man cares about you enough to ask about your relationship goals and asks you to enter into a committed relationship with him. If a man asks invasive questions, keep your lip zipped and steer the conversation to neutral topics, like metaphysics or the weather.

Love Script

You're out eating linguini, when all of a sudden your date casually says, "So, are you dating anyone else, Angela?"

Lob back: "Well, I'm dating, but it's nothing serious."

This is a line poached from men themselves! And it works. Even if you aren't dating anyone it makes you sound desirable, sets a boundary, and protects your privacy.

Or try this elegant one-liner: "I'm single at the moment."

If he keeps pressing, say, "That info is on a need to know basis, bud!"

Never let a man press you for more information than he's earned. Until a man's ready to commit, and you are too, all he needs to know is that you like him enough to keep dating him and enjoying your clams.

ROMANTIC RULE: *Your exclusivity is a privilege that a man must earn. Knowledge about your calendar should remain top secret until a commitment is made.*

The Secret Bargaining Power of Your Exclusivity

Imagine you owned a lovely home on a piece of prime real estate. You watered the lawn, manicured the bushes, painted the interior, and put the house on the market. You'd never sell it at a rock bottom price, fearing that no one else would make an offer. Instead, you'd wait for decent offers from multiple buyers, and only close the deal when you got the proposal that you really wanted, maybe for even *more* than you wanted.

Unless you have severely undervalued your hot property!

REALITY CHECK: The Romantic Researcher always applies the 'sellers' market theory' to her relationships.

Question: Would you only show your property to a buyer who wasn't sure he really wanted to live there? Even if he said he liked it, even *loved* it, but wasn't quite ready to buy *(because he secretly thought that he'd find something better)*? And while he was "finding himself and "figuring things out," you agreed to refuse to take bids from other buyers. Instead, you put the property on hold for him indefinitely, let him live in it for free, gave away your cats because he was allergic to them . . . *and slept with him, too!*

If this sounds way too familiar, you've probably fallen for—and into—a terrible time-wasting trap more commonly known as **Serial Monogamy.**

> **SERIAL MONOGAMY** v. You voluntarily commit yourself to a string of relationships that fail to yield long-term commitment, marriage, or family. You (unwisely) agree to open-ended monogamy in the hopes that men will step up if you just love 'em enough.* You agree to take yourself off the market for a man who's not ready to fully commit to you because you're either (a) having amazing sex with him, or (b) he mentioned that he wanted to get married "someday" when you went hiking together.

You hang in there until you realize that you're wasting your time, and then do it all over again, with someone new.

---

* This is like offering men an uncollateralized loan of your emotional capital.

NEWSFLASH : The typical male has no reason to believe that being a "boyfriend" for long stretches of time is actually a problem. And it isn't, for him. Men can have children when they're sixty. Who wouldn't want to keep the audition process going as long as possible if they could get away with it? Men love No-Time-Frame Dating because if you agree to it, they don't have to worry about competing for you with other men. When you give up your exclusivity without clear terms, they get the luxury of taking you out of the field and keeping you in "audition mode" indefinitely. No-Time-Frame Dating allows men to date you, have sex with you, even be monogamous with you, and still never marry you! This is exactly how we let men take minimum risks while receiving maximum pleasure.

ROMANTIC RULE: *Always prequalify your Love Birds to see if they have a real emotional investment in your relationship before taking yourself off the market, and get rid of the ones who are just browsing.*

Healthy relationships are mergers between two partners whose terms should be negotiated up front. In days of yore, marriage was a looked upon as a business contract between two families. Thankfully, our fathers don't have to bribe men with dowries to marry us anymore. Now the men are supposed to commit to us for free *(for the love of us)*. When women don't speak up, they passively supply what *men* want, by default.

If you keep winding up on your knees *instead of the other way around*, you're probably using the outmoded. **On a Wing and a Prayer Man Plan.**

ON A WING AND A PRAYER MAN PLAN v. You cross your fingers and just "go with the flow," in the hopes that things will magically work out if you leave things up to chance (aka your boyfriend).

REALITY CHECK: When you refuse to speak up, it'll only be the luck of the draw if you find a man who's emotionally mature enough, reckless enough, or psychic enough to provide exactly you what you want. That's why it's so important to know exactly what your dating requirements are, and communicate them in language even a man can understand.

Mantra: Negotiations begin today!

Romantic Researchers, Remember

- It's not whom you've been dating but how you've been dating that's the problem.

- Dating isn't a mini-relationship, it's a pleasurable fact-finding mission.

- Dating is a process that always results in The Survival of the Fittest when you wisely follow the laws of natural selection.

- Flock Consciousness is the antidote to the endless dating trap!

A Bird in the Hand Is Worth Two in the Bush

Do not squander time. That is the stuff life is made of.

–Gone With the Wind

If you're wise, you'll *never bring up the topic of exclusivity with a man ever again.* You'll wait for him to bring it up with you, instead.

ROMANTIC RULE: *Always let men press you for exclusivity, and not the other way around.*

When men fall in love, they'll pressure you for a commitment of monogamy all by themselves, usually right *after* they start having sex with you. They'll want to make sure that you'll refuse sexual invitations from other available males. For men, getting you to agree to monogamy can be translated thusly: *"I won't cheat, if you don't!"* or *"I'd like to put you on hold and figure out how I feel about you somewhere down the road."*

Agreeing to this sloppy arrangement is exactly how many women lose years of their lives to Mr. Wrong, who seemed so very right at the outset! When women fail to specify how much time they'll be willing to invest in an exclusive relationship before seeing their long-term goals accomplished, they often wind up spinning their wheels with inappropriate men. Or allow relationships with Love Birds capable of pair-bonding to drift.

Note: If you're very young or just up for some fun, you may choose to wing it,* too. But if you're ready to roost, please pay close attention to this:

MAN FACT: *Once a man asks for your exclusivity, it's your cue to quickly negotiate the terms of your surrender!*

THE PECKING ORDER PRINCIPLE: *A woman should never surrender her exclusivity until a man offers a relationship whose terms and conditions are truly acceptable. Resist the temptation to give up your exclusivity until someone has given you a very good reason to do so.*

---

* Commit to an exclusive, monogamous No-Time-Frame-Dating kind of relationship.

Step One: Separate the Men from the Boys

When a man asks you for your exclusivity, you'll need to:

1. Make sure he has compatible relationship goals
2. Set a time limit with him about how long you'll be willing to "test drive" your relationship.

Love Script

Start by communicating your personal relationship goals to him in a simple sentence or two: ***"I'd love to see more of you, Humphrey. But you should know that I'm looking for*** [marriage, family, an open relationship]. ***And you?"***

WARNING: If this sentence rubbed him the wrong way or seems to come as something of shock, you can choose to drop him, or keep him incubating in your flock. But beware the Lame Duck who flaps around and doesn't meet your conversation halfway. If you spot him in your midst, have a little fun with him like this: *"I hope you want a big family, Jack, because I sure do. Twins run in my family!"*

Gulp!

Step Two: Throw Salt on His Tail

If he chirps back in agreement that his goals are compatible with yours, Bravo! Take this bird at his word. Now you'll need to clearly state what the expiration date on your "exclusive offer" is.

Love Script
"I'm thrilled that you want to move things forward with me Richard, but you should know that I'd only be comfortable being

exclusive for [six months, nine months, one year] *before we got engaged, pregnant, married.*

WARNING: Upon hearing this statement uttered by you, men will (predictably) start squawking about how they don't want to feel "pressured" into (*engagement, marriage, pregnancy*) and start singing the Battle Hymn of the (Male) Republic: *"What? Wait a minute! How can you expect me know after only one month of dating you if or when I'll feel like* [proposing, getting pregnant, buying a home]? *I hate being pressured! My last girlfriend tried to try to pressure me and I broke up with her."*

When he starts trilling this predictable little tune, don't go into a tailspin. Simply defy his flighty logic with a little dose of reality: "I understand you don't want to feel pressured, Rich. But what about me? My time frame needs to be considered too. I'm not saying that you have to propose to me in nine months. All I'm saying is, that's how much time I'd be comfortable exclusively dating you, to see if things are working out between us."

This logic is very hard, dare I day *near impossible,* for a man to refute. You've told him that while you respect his time frame, he'll need to respect *yours* too. So zip your lip and observe him. He's either going to fly straight into the windowpane, or do laps in big slow circles and come up with a snappy comeback.

"Hey, I've been faithful to you since the day we met, but if there's someone else you'd rather date, I won't stand in your way!"

He might even throw in a cocky *"I'm not worried about the competition anyway."*

If he's a deep thinker -or a lawyer- he might try to manipulate you like this: *"I think that the best kind of relationship is when two people are monogamous because they* want *to be, not because they* need *to be, or a piece of paper says that they* have *to be!"*

If you hear this adolescent tune, quickly take the air out of his sails this way: *"Are you really all right with me dating other people,*

Dick? If that's the case, it's okay, but you should know it'll change the way that I continue to date you." At this point, your bird will probably start turning green and ask in a tight little voice what in God's name you mean.

MAN FACT: *All men are like Icarus. They don't know they're flying too close to the sun until you bring them back down to earth.*

So, call his blustery bluff thusly: *"Well, I'd probably see you no more that once or twice a week, max. And I may decide to continue sleeping with you. I certainly wouldn't be on the phone with you every day."*

Do not utter one more word! You've seen him, raised him, called him (and cornered him!) into showing you his hand. Men who have real partnership potential will now fold, back down, knock it off, grow up, and ante up. (Set a time frame that's fair for the both of you.) *C'est magnifique!* You've taught him a wonderful trick called Stepping on Command.

Note: Write this date in your calendar. Then follow the instructions on page 221 one month prior to it.

If you find, however, that your bird starts to balk, behaves like a Bat out of Hell, or resists this talk, don't become alarmed. He may need a little space to contemplate his (bleak) future without you. Don't cave in! Hold your ground. Men who aren't sociopaths (aka womanizers) will often have a complete change of heart within several days a month, or even two months. If you wait him out he may have a total turnabout. But he doesn't, please don't fret or pout! Don't despair! Don't eat inexpensive chocolates, or start tearing out your hair.

MAN FACT *Selfish and immature men run from emotional accountability as fast as they can.*

Let Peter Pan fly out the window, and go find yourself a man!

You Should Only Surrender
Your Exclusivity to a Man When . . .

1. You've thoroughly qualified your Lovebird.

2. He says he shares the same relationship goals that you do and is committed to realizing them with you.

3. You both have a time frame in which to accomplish them.

Then you can date him exclusively with your conscience clear. Nice job on the fancy footwork, my dear!

seventeen

The Birds and the Bees

We're not above birds; let's misbehave!

–Cole Porter

Women bait and men desperately try to catch. It's genetic. When a woman understands that men really do love the hunt, she isn't actually *cockteasing* but agreeably encouraging a predatory chase. That's why it's always a good idea to prolong the make-out phase of your relationship before flinging open Pandora's box. Here's to the noble art of keeping your eyes open and your thong on!

The Cocktease (aka the Artful Dodger)

Mysterious, barbaric, and arcane — what more needs to be said about the art of female seduction? What more . . . other than it's also beautiful. And that, like other pastimes involving the pursuit of game for pleasure, it's rich with contradictions.

Q: What's the average number of dates you go on before going all the way?

One date? Two dates? Three dates? More than five?

According to the Nobel laureates at *Cosmo*, 55 percent of the respondents answered three dates. Bluntly put, men and women both seem to agree that it's three strikes, they're out, or three dates, he's in!

Unfortunately, this courtship schedule is far too brief for most women to conduct anything resembling proper "research." Unless your male is going to be just a plaything, the wise manhandler always benefits by artfully cockteasing a man first before diving completely undercover.

ROMANTIC RULE: *Don't have casual sex with a man whom you're falling for until he's falling in love with you, too.*

Pheromones and Oxytocin:
The Twin Chemistry Set Called Love

Sex doesn't make men fall in love with you. Love makes men fall in love with you. But sex helps!

–Lauren Frances, Ph. DD

Irritating Fact: Mother Nature wisely predicted that women would never tolerate the bad habits of most men, so she decided to drug us to ensure the propagation of the species. She gave us a "cuddle hormone" called oxytocin that bonds us instantly to any man with whom we have even passable sex. And once they make us orgasm, our goose is cooked no matter how much we may have despised them before they got our thong off. Then, the more sex you have with this fiend, the more bonded you'll become, until just seeing him, smelling him, or finding his crumpled shirt in your laundry basket will chemically activate you with rapturous feelings of love and make you want to put up with him long enough to impregnate you (seems to be Mother Nature's reasoning here).

Much More Irritating Fact: Men possess this hormone, too, but in such ridiculously small amounts that it isn't enough to produce the desire for monogamy.*

Mother Nature was afraid that women, drugged or not, would find men too smelly and irritating to keep indoors, so she came up with a little backup plan. She gave men a *completely different* genetic primal directive: *"Go forth, young harem master, and get your freak on. Cast your seed upon the many and avoid capture!"*

This explains why it takes men so much more time to emotionally connect to women (from their dick to the brain and then to the heart), and also explains why they violently resist enemy capture (monogamy). They're actually fighting against Mother Nature herself!

ROMANTIC RULE: *Men like to think of their bodies as a temple, with a lot of worshippers.*

Men will try to get into your panties *first* and conduct important relationship research *second*. And if they do emotionally step up after sex, always pay very close attention because, unlike you (the love-drugged), they're falling for you stone-cold sober!

Once men swoop you up in their big sexy talons, they'll try to get as physically close to you as two separate people can who aren't Siamese twins. He may also, however, fly right out the window after he finishes ravishing you (the come-and-go migratory pattern).

Birds of prey fall in love over time by actively pursuing you, thinking about you when you're apart, and *then* having sex with you (aka hunting). By artfully cockteasing a man, you do him *such* a favor . . . you give him the space he needs to have a feeling reach two feet higher than his belt buckle!

---

* Sadly, I did not make this up!

ROMANTIC RULE: *Getting him hard won't make his heart soft, but falling in love with you over time will.*

> *The cocktease takes one step forward and two tiny steps back to inflame a man's desire. The rogue will make a valiant attempt to seduce her, but denied an easy victory, he redoubles his efforts. Although a man may get into a pet at being denied his quick pleasure, he'll love nothing more than this sweet torment. His manhood will be completely at the ready! So after he makes proper oaths of fealty, allow him his spoils . . . and let him rip the bodice from your heaving bosom.*
>
> *—The Confessions of Dr. L*

Slowing men down gives them a wonderful opportunity to realize that you're more than just a bunny snack. Don't let him devour you right away. Make him do it for *hours and hours* over the course of several weeks at least! Rediscover the kiss, and I promise you this: When you make out in restaurants, bars, and the front seats of cars, or up against the wall in the hall . . . *he'll want to rip your panties off with his teeth.*

ROMANTIC RULE: *Don't go into a sex coma until you've thoroughly fact-checked your man, administered verbal truth serum, and quizzed him like a pro.*

MANHANDLING MANEUVER: *Perform these interrogations while wearing black leather boots and gloves, and if he passes your test, keep 'em on when everything else comes off.*

How to Keep Your Man on Simmer

When you need to slow a man down, here's a useful tip: Don't invite him in, until you're ready to invite him *all* the way in.

MAN FACT: *Once you let men indoors, they just want to get naked.*

LOVE STOVE

Here are two basic facts about the breeding habits of the typical sexually stimulated male:

1. Men will have sex anywhere, be it a tool shed, a pool shed, or aisles S through V at your local library. Your first several dates should be in public places, and end on your doorstep. Once you bring men indoors, they're liable to raise the roof by crowing like Rowdy Roosters before sunrise. (*See* Woodpecker.)

2. Giving a man "sex to remember you by" doesn't make him want you more, but thinking about ravishing you upon his return certainly will!

Male Breeding Manners and the Two-for-One Rule

Men need to learn how to wait their turn, especially since their turn requires so little encouragement, once it finally comes up. This is the real logic behind the seemingly arcane practices of chivalry that are alive and well today. Helping you on with your coat, opening your car door, and walking behind you while exiting a restaurant. Mastering chivalrous good manners are a kind of "sex prep" for young males brilliantly designed to train men to come second, and not first, in the bedroom.

MAN FACT: *Men shouldn't think about satisfying themselves till they've made their girlfriends see godhead (orgasm) at least once.* *

Twice is *definitely* better and is the gentlemen's rule of thumb. Besides, as any good lover knows, once you get a girl going, she'll go all night. Never feel bad if your man is slaving away. Hard work is good for them . . . and besides, if you make them do their duty, *maybe they'll get better at it.*

To quote Mike Dugan: Women don't take longer . . . women last longer!

Always insist on the Two-for-One Rule.

Deciphering Primal Male Sexual Sign Language

Here are two common hand signals that you'll need a heads-up about . . . before you start to go down.

Tommy, Can You Feel Me?

Does this sound familiar? You're making out with a man, when all of a sudden he reaches over, grabs your hand, and just puts it on his dick (which is now the size of a baseball bat). Even if you were deaf, dumb, and blind, it would be impossible to miss.

Most women have been on the receiving end of this gesture, but some of you may be confused as to its meaning. Allow me to clarify it for you, and yes, you may borrow my pen.

---

* Don't fake!

This is the international mating signal in every language for "Our make-out is now over. We are going to the next level. I hope I brought a condom!"

It's just like baking. Once the yeast has risen, it's biscuits, baby. He'll want to show you the size of his rolling pin.

WARNING: Men who are well endowed often do this as a preview of what's to come. *Literally.* Unless you are really ready to go all the way, right now, you had best remove your hand immediately and back away from it. He has now switched into "Need-to-Breed mode," and you're asking for trouble if you try to make him "behave," regain his composure, and go back in time to the 1950s. Once your hand is on his dick, he'll think there is absolutely no reason to turn back the hands of time and just "make out" again!

MAN FACT: Men like to move forward and not backward, in wartime campaigns and in the sack.

Decent men want you to feel comfortable. They don't stop dating women who set reasonable limits. They don't really expect you to give them exactly what they want, when they want it. Good guys invest the time that it takes for the both of you to get on the same page when they're really interested in you.

Men *will* get mad if you purposely confuse them (saying yes and then no and then yes and then no), or unfairly insisting that they sexually reset their c(l)ock to pre-make-out position.

Translation: Bitch.

Soothing the Savage Bird

Follow these five easy steps to soothe the savage beast:

1. Simply remove your hand and say, "*Whoa, I am soooo thirsty. I'll be back in a jiffy.*"

2. Exit the room and give him a minute to regain his composure.

3. Return and say, *"Mmmmnn . . . here's some nice cold water."*

4. If he tries to pick up right where he left off, say, *"Baby, I'm so flattered, but I'm not quite ready to go there yet. Can we slow down a little? I need to catch my breath!"*

5. Don't sit down again! He'll get the message. Simply open the door, have a good-night peck, and say, *"I'd really love to see you again,"* then shoo him right out the door.

ROMANTIC RULE: *Respect the dick. Immediately back away from it and don't continue to handle it, if you're not ready to rock it.*

Got it?

Note: While there are more than six thousand languages in the world, all men still use "primal sexual sign language."

Proof: Evolution is a mere blip in the mind of God.

The Handyman:
How to Keep Him at Bay

The next hand signal that unruly men often employ is wonderfully illustrated in this field study conducted by a colleague, Katarina. Katarina is a curvaceous brunette and full of fun. Here's how she wrangled a randy handyman . . . it's ingenious.

Case Study

"I once dated an action-adventure film director whom we'll call 'the Handyman.' Even though he had a terrible reputation for screaming on the set and womanizing, he seemed nice enough at first. I was newly single and thought, 'Oh, what the hell?' I was up for some fun.

"We went out and everything seemed perfect, until I noticed, to my dismay, that while we were making out, *he had his hand in his pants*. On a first date, I found this to be outrageous behavior. He wanted action all right, and I was unable to say, 'Cut.'

"When he didn't stop, I couldn't help but feel insulted. I mean, what was I, chopped liver? He said he was 'too turned on' to stop. Well, okay, I thought. Good excuse. The next time we went out (yeah, I know, I'm an idiot) I wore a scarf just in case. And when the Handyman started to reach for his gun, I was ready. I looked him in the eye and said, 'Hold out your hands, mister!' and then whipped the scarf from my neck and tied his hands quickly together. I then proceeded to kiss him.

"This drove him wild, and it was really fun until he started begging me to untie him. To my dismay his hand went right back to his remote. He was madly in love with it and refused to keep his hands off it. When I finally said, 'Hey, bud! What about me? I'm feeling a little left out over here,' he snapped, 'It's not tit for tat! I'll take care of you next time.' *Next time?* As if! I fired him instantly."

eighteen

Sex and the Single Bird

The Farmer in the Dell:
How to Initiate a Conversation about STDs and Safe Sex

You must always guard your eggs like a farmer in the dell. The very best way to protect yourself is to be exclusive, go to the same doctor, and then get tested for everything under the sun, *together*. But if you're in the first flush and in more of a rush, the easiest way to discuss barnyard complaints is as simple as this: *Before* you're in any danger of contracting something, say, "Do you have anything I'm not going to want to catch?"

Hear him out. And then it's your turn. If you're both magically STD free, you *still* have to use a condom until you're sexually exclusive with each other. It's always chivalrous if the man comes prepared to "cloak his dagger." But if he isn't prepared, you should be. Always BYOB (Bring Your Own Birth Control) and then remember to use it!

MAN FACT: *Men will try to escape wearing a condom about as fast as a cat getting out of a collar.*

Use the following love scripts to exert Vulcan (vaginal) mind control over men when they're attempting to avoid plastic capture:

If he tries: "I'm not that kind of guy. I don't just carry them around in my wallet."
Quip back: "Well, I must be that kind of girl because I've got one in my purse!"

"I forgot to bring them."
"Well, there's a 7-Eleven right down the street. And grab me a Diet Coke while you're at it."

"I can't feel anything! I want to take it off!"
"Well, maybe we shouldn't have sex. Wanna go to the movies?"

"Please, baby, you're so hot, I just can't stop!"
"Okay, down boy! Sit! Stay. Now put this condom on or I'm putting my panties on, Ron."

"I can't get hard wearing one."
"No problem. Let's take some Viagra together. It's amazing."

"I always use one, so I'm safe."
"Wow. What a relief. But if you want to have sex with me, you still need to put on a slipcover."

"Just once, baby, please?"
"Nope. If you want some love, put on a sex mitten, Tom."

"I won't come, I promise I won't come!"
"Aren't you thoughtful! But even if you don't come, you still need to wear a raincoat."

"I'm totally safe; I was tested two months ago."
"I'm glad you're keeping tabs on things. But we need to use protection if you want to get near me with your erection!"

WARNING: Only guys most likely to have STDs use lines like the following:

> "Why? I don't have any STDs!"
> *"Boy, am I relieved! Let's slip on this penis protector. It looks just about your size."*

> "I never use one!"
> *"Wow. Let's be friends."*

> "I won't have sex with you then."
> *"Finally we agree on something. I'm going to the movies. Ciao."*

MAN FACT: *If a man wants to have sex with you without a condom, he's sleeping with everybody else without one, too!*

nineteen

Male Breeding Displays

Now let's review the sexual displays of the modern breeding male, and some manhandling tips that you won't want to miss!

Early Birds

Some men — sexual narcissists, selfish Lame Ducks, and most eighteen-year-olds — have a nasty habit of being Early Birds. Many Early Birds mistakenly think that just because they're climaxing, you are too, and now *everybody's happy*. Unfortunately, the Early Bird will go right on thinking that you're satisfied unless you correctly train him to put *your* orgasm before his own, which, as we have discussed, is exactly where it should be. This is the real reason why Mother Nature blessed strapping young men and forty-year-old women with identical sex drives . . . so he'd receive the instruction that he so desperately needs from a woman he'll actually *listen* to.

ROMANTIC RULE: *Never pretend to be having a ball when you aren't.*

A laissez-faire attitude about your own orgasm is passive negative reinforcement. It lulls men into thinking that their inadequate mating habits are actually satisfying, trains them to be lazy and selfish in the sack, and leaves the problem for the next girl to deal with. Come on, people!

How to Slow Down Your Early Bird

The next time he's racing you to the finish line, slow him down by whispering, "Baby, make me wait," softly in his ear, and then repeat this instruction several times, if necessary. Always look at him with meaning and smile seductively as you say it. You'll be able to tell when the light goes on because his rhythm will automatically slow down and he'll look at you like the first caveman kindling a fire. Et voilà! Now we're getting somewhere.

Give him a wicked little grin as a reward, and encourage him to stay the course and slow his pace by repeatedly telling him how good it feels, how big he is, how hot he's making you, blah, blah, blah . . . you know the drill. Men need repeated verbal encouragement while being sexually retrained, so always praise your bird when he's trying very hard to please you.

If that didn't make an impression, shout, "Darling, the train is moving but I'm not onboard! Slow down! You've got to make my whistle blow before you leave the station."

This will be so confusing he'll come to a complete halt and stop right in his tracks, I promise you that.

MAN FACT: *Remember, nice guys finish last.*

Dominant Crowing Cocks

This rowdy rooster has quite a lot to crow about. He's the master of the multiple orgasm. You may accidentally hyperventilate from excitement, so put the paramedics on speed dial . . . just in case of emergencies.

Because they are sex geniuses, Crowing Cocks can usually mate with females as often as they like and still hope to spread their genes far and wide. Hopefully, for your sake, your Cock will be of the rare monogamous variety, but any man this good in the sack probably got this way because he's had so much practice boning up.

Typically, a Crowing Cock displays his sexual supremacy by quickly putting his chick into a "sex coma." This is usually done in an attempt at *relationship intervention.* He's hoping you'll be so impressed by his outstanding sexual performance that you'll jump on his erect manhood, go right into a sex coma, and completely forget to have a boundary with him. And he'll usually be right. It will be damned near impossible to imagine how you ever lived without him by the time he's done with you, and he knows it.

If you have a Crowing Cock in your flock, congrats! He's a wonderful addition and can be enjoyed like any fun, forbidden food. Don't forget that this man is, more often than not, just a treat and shouldn't take the place of dinner. But if, in the course of your research, you discover that he's prime for the plucking, too, you'll have hit the jackpot. Who'll be the one crowing then? Why, I think it'll be *you.*

The Master Cock: Predatory Sex Addicts

Polygamous despots of ancient times have a lot in common with Master Cocks. These adulterous males act like they're single even when they're married. Farmers (and girlfriends) have always known that over time, Master Cocks grow less interested in mating repeatedly with the same hen. But when a new female is introduced, our Cock wants to copulate, and he allocates considerably more sperm to his new mate.

WARNING: This heartthrob is impossible to pin down unless you physically tie him down (he'll probably suggest you use handcuffs). He's also erratic and dangerous, but this may only add to his allure. Your love affair will feel like you're watching a traffic accident happen in slow motion, but you won't try to put on the brakes because he's so ridiculously hot.

The only way to date a Master Cock is to treat him exactly the way that he treats you: like an illicit tryst at an expensive hotel, or motel, depending on his budget.

Once you're hooked (bedded), he won't have time to see you. He's the master of avoidance and will quickly put you into romantic rotation. He's on tour, on the set, in the studio, or on vacation with the wife. And hunting for more groupies to feed his predatory appetite.

The only way to get over him is to go cold turkey and find a Dodo Bird or immediately buy a vibrator (or both) to expedite your emotional healing.

To lure him, wear a belly shirt and head toward the back of the barn. He'll be surrounded by a gaggle of very hot chicks. Cock-a-doodle-doo, baby!

The Dead Duck

The Dead Duck has a disturbing condition known as "equipment failure." If his little soldier won't stand at attention right away, don't panic. The most experienced researchers often ignore poor posture altogether if it occurs during a first or second engagement in the field. Sometimes the "little general" needs a few skirmishes before taking the hill, so I always advise allowing men a few trial runs before calling in the cavalry.

To resurrect a dead duck, put him at ease by complimenting his lovely touch and his gorgeous brown eyes, which sear right into the depths of your very soul. Don't comment on his package being MIA, and give him two more chances, if you like him. He probably suffered temporary performance anxiety because you were so damned hot, and he'll soon get over the bump and hump you soon enough.

If he disappoints you three times, however, you're dealing with a psycho/medical problem, and he should be thoughtful enough to stop annoying you and go get the magic from a bottle . . . (Viagra). In this day and age there is absolutely *no excuse* for a man to be this inconsiderate. It'd be like a woman refusing to wax her undercarriage before date night. But, oh, a slumping soldier is so much worse!

ROMANTIC RULE: *When playing with balls, it's one, two, three strikes, he's out!*

Now, some will say that all a man needs to be a great lay are two fingers and some determination.

Fact: The only people who ever say this are men! Every gal wants a raging hard-on. After all . . .

even Mother Nature believes in survival of the stiffest!

Note: A Dead Duck will often refuse to take V to handle his package, and act like it's an affront to his manhood. He may sulk, or even try to pretend that it's *your* fault that he can't perform. We scoff at this! He's definitely the problem, not you, and everybody knows it.

PC Rebuttal: Some would say that if a woman doesn't want to be judged by the size of her thighs, she has no right to judge a man who's having trouble maintaining a hard-on. If you're feeling guilty, ponder this . . . *you can still have sex with him no matter what size your ass is!*

MANHANDLING MANEUVER: *The best technique for handling a Dead Duck is to offer to take Viagra with him. Now, before you get your nose out of joint, consider this: It's no different than walking a youngster to the school bus and helping him get onboard. Viagra is known to have sexually stimulating properties for the ladies, too, and will often result in some earth-shattering orgasms! I took it once and thought I was going to have a heart attack, but I'm already fast . . .*

Wait. . . . That didn't sound right. Must rewrite.

Ask your physician for some Viagra samples (don't be nervous, they'll make sympathetic clucking noises), and the next time you and your Dead Duck are together, lean in and suggest with a conspiratorial grin that you both take some V. He'll think it's kinky. Then you can have a little revival meeting lying down. He can thank Jesus, and you can praise the Lord!

Note: Find out if he has a heart condition *before* he takes it unless you're already in the will. (*See* Anna Nicole.)

The Lucky Duck

The Lucky Duck is *any* guy lucky enough to bed you, hon!

Seductive Crooning and Cooing

When men are aroused, they will say almost anything. That is why they are verbally armed and potentially dangerous. They've been dragged to enough chick flicks and have seen enough DeBeers commercials to know exactly which utterances will make you want to trust them with your nakedness.

Seductive Cooing

- "I've always had a crush on you but I thought you'd never go out with me."
- "I feel so comfortable with you it's scary."
- "You remind me of the only woman I've ever loved."
- "I've never been able to talk to anybody the way I can talk to you."
- "I want you to meet my mother."
- "You'd look gorgeous pregnant."

MAN FACT: *Men know exactly what women want to hear. This is where the old adage "If his lips are moving . . . he's lying" comes from.*

Also ignore declarations made during sex, like "Let's get married." "I love you." "Let's go to the Bahamas."

The things that a man blurts out during sex are like the deranged rantings of drunkards. He'll usually plead temporary insanity or deny any knowledge of his agitated warbling when he finally comes . . . to.

MAN FACT: *If your lover makes the same declarations in the light of day, he actually meant them!*

How to Lure a Dodo

If Mr. Right has become your Nemesis Bird, Mr. Right now can be such a boon! Here are some tips to lure a Dodo, and let him know you're in the mood.

> **FOOLING AROUND** *v* 1. having sex with someone who's gorgeous but just too dumb to love. 2. the perfect "go-to" man-management package preferred by the newly single woman just released back into the field, or the too-busy-to-give-a-hoot working woman, or any gal who's just up for fun.

Love Script to Lure the Dodo

Say with enthusiasm: *"I'm not looking for anything serious right now. I hope you don't mind. I'm just up for some fun."* This statement sends a clear message that you're emotionally unavailable and up for a romp. *"Have you ever had sex in a Land Cruiser?"* will always work too!

Beware: Using these come-hither lines will inspire such enthusiasm, you may wind up with a mandicap.

MANDICAP 1. sex-related injury. 2. usage: As in, "He rode me so hard he gave me a mandicap! I need a bag of frozen peas and a nice long nap."

Clipping His Wings:
Naughty Things Men Try to Get Away With and What You Can Do About It

Men nowadays request the most wildly debauched behavior from women whom they barely know with a totally straight face. These men are winging it and trying to see how much they can get away with, so never feel pressured to say yes (unless you really, really want to!). Use the following tips to deflect unwelcome sexual advances from the devilishly deviant Dirty Bird.

The Boyfriend Exchange Program
(aka Swinging or Partner Swapping)

This occurs when your boyfriend wants to have sex with your best friend and doesn't want to cheat or do the hard work of convincing her *himself*. He wants you to do it for him.

The Upside: The Boyfriend Exchange Program is like getting to wear a sweater without taking off the tags for easy returns!

Q: Is it better to swap partners with someone you know or someone you don't know?

A: Unless you do a lot of catalog shopping, I'd definitely recommend knowing the person first. You probably know what looks good on you, and who'd look good on you, so I recommend that you take charge of the casting.

To Deflect: If your man asks if you'd ever consider having a ménage à trois with your gal pal, say: *"When Betsey remembers to return my Jell-O mold, I'll consider it. But until then, I'm not lending her my boyfriend!"*

Three Answers for Threeways: *

> HIM: *Have you had a threesome before?*
> YOU: *1. Does the cat count?*
> *2. I had to give it up. Someone always feels left out and it's never me!*
> *3. Oh darling, I'm sure you'll do just fine. You're not only funny, you're so thoughtful, too!*

ROMANTIC RULE: *Always remember that good etiquette dictates that if you swap up, remember to swap back or you'll go from being a swapper to a swiper . . . and that's bad manners!*

Home Videos

This is the audiovisual version of the old notch on the belt (and the makings of future blackmail). Guys who want to photograph you for posterity usually wind up showing your posterior to their friends over a beer. These tapes can and probably will be used against you. If you start your own do-it-at-home porn dynasty, always make sure *you* keep the videos and destroy them right after you watch 'em with your girlfriends.

---

* This course is often given in France and on American college campuses. (*See* "Unexplained Lesbianism and the Jell-O Shot.")

To Deflect: Say, *"We can make one on our honeymoon."*
Remember to make him sign a waiver.

Dressing Up and Role-Playing

I think everyone should get spanked by Santa at least *once* in a lifetime.

SPANKER *n* 1. one who spanks.

To Deflect: (Hmm . . . I can't think of one good reason not to try this on for size. Ummm. Wow. I'm stumped. Work on this later.)

Tip: If you're on your knees begging for mercy, remember to wear stilettos!

Backdoor Love

This request is a fave of the Bat Out of Hell and the Dirty Bird.

Request: *"Baby, can we do it from behind?"*

Rebuttal: *"Darling, I think a girl's got to save something for the honeymoon, don't you?"*

Tip: If a man asks you to engage in this practice, it's always wise to pretend it's your first time!

twenty

Flight Patterns

"Ah, madam," said Lancelot sadly, "I love you only
and no other woman in all the world. But for many reasons
I strive to flee your presence."

–Arthurian Legend

 The "flight" response is at the root of a man's need for emotional "space." Depending on the man, his flight patterns may look like short jaunts or long-term adventures.

After several months of gathering data, a pattern should emerge and you'll be able to predict your bird's migration routes and favorite escape pathways.

The Evolution of the Escapee Boyfriend

Modern men are walking around with the same hormonal responses to imminent danger as cavemen. When men perceive a threat to their freedom, their bodies prepare to fight to the death or take flight to escape certain defeat by a superior adversary . . . you. This primal fight-or-flight instinct usually causes an alarmed man to turn tail and flee. So don't blame yourself; it's genetic!

He Flew the Coop

You've been dating intensely for a while and every time you look over your shoulder, he's always right . . . *what?* Wait a minute, where did he go? Uh-oh, sound familiar?

You've just experienced the most frustrating (and mysterious) of all male dating phenoms. You were both on cloud nine but now he needs some "space."

SPACE *n* 1. spaced, or spacing you out. 2. the universe beyond the earth's atmosphere. 3. common male need after prolonged intimacy with a woman. Usage: "I need some space."

You're confused. You thought everything was perfect. So what happened?

Ongoing intimacy with women often triggers the male self-preservation directive: Fly low, drop cargo! Your proximity has inadvertently triggered his primal need to fly toward freedom. He longs to soar over the tundra, survey the glorious world unencumbered by emotional baggage *(you)*, and feel the rush of air under his wings. And to look for tiny mice.

Don't worry. After he reassures himself that he's still capable of flight, he'll grow tired of flapping around and land on your doorstep once again, if he loves you. Or if he was really, really into having sex with you.

When he returns, the wise manhandler won't take his need for space personally. She'll calmly say, "Hi hon." *Translation:* I left the cleaver in the kitchen.

MANHANDLING MANEUVER: *You'll score huge bonus points (25!) for not chopping his head off. If he apologizes, tell him, "No problem, I'll just take it out in trade . . . in the bedroom." This will cause him to spontaneously erupt with an appreciative "You're so awesome. Come here baby," accompanied by a heartfelt salute below the belt.*

The Wild Goose Chase

All men have an inner GPS (Girl Positioning System), which allows them to locate and migrate toward or away from their targeted prey. They also use it to spot and flee from dangerous predators, irritating girlfriends, or angry exes.

Most men are masters at resisting "emotional arrest." When things get too heavy, they try to fly away, just to see if they still can.

ROMANTIC RULE: *Don't ever bar the door and prevent a man who's trying to flee your presence from taking flight.*

This will only backfire on you. Screaming, crying, vase throwing, and threatening suicide, homicide, or patricide are misguided attempts at manhandling, and you'll pay a huge price for any victory you *think* you've won. Men abhor women who don't respect their right to leave an apartment, conversation, or relationship if they so choose. When men start singing "Freebird," just open the door and let 'em fly away. You can always lock it after them!

If you make a scene every time your man needs space, he'll feel smothered and controlled and look for *even more* ways to flee the relationship. You'll teach him to mistrust you and cause him to become agitated, angry, or passive-aggressive. He may even become sneaky and plotting or downright hostile. Let him go. Once he does a couple of laps, he'll satisfy his urge and return to you refreshed, attentive, *and human*. So retract your claws and purr.

Short-Looped Migration Pattern
(aka Why Did the Chicken Cross the Road?)

Sometimes men will fly the coop to reassure themselves that they haven't become totally pussy-whipped . . . I mean, domesticated. This is known as a short-looped migration or, in lay terms, poker night.

He majestically surveys the terrain, has a beer, and then flies home. There was nothing in particular that he wanted anyway; he simply needed to get some air, stretch his legs, and prove to himself that the cage door was still open. Sometimes this short jaunt takes only twenty minutes. He'll make a quick run to the store, take the dog for a walk, or make a quick trip to the local watering hole and come right back home. Unless he's drinking Wild Turkey.

Winged Migration
(aka Eccentric Migrations)

The typical American bachelor party is a perfect example of an "eccentric migration." Birds may travel considerable distances from their usual nesting areas (your place) to predictable partying destinations (Vegas!) where they spend several flightless days in drunken revelry.

These debauched migrations lead them pell-mell into the breeding ranges of some scandalously underdressed females. Don't worry, stripper chicks don't want him, they want a tip! So leave them alone and they'll come home, dragging their tailfeathers behind 'em.

The Come and Go Migration

You threw caution to the winds because you couldn't imagine ever taking him seriously, so you thought, "Screw it," or because he was so damned hot you didn't want to resist. And now you're looking at the telephone and wondering when he'll call.

MAN FACT: *A guy who's flying at warp speed five knows that this is much too fast. He's walking a fine line between hot fun and bad manners. Although this can be delightful in the moment, so is eating an entire box of chocolates.*

Strange but true male factoid: Men are more uncomfortable with one-night stands than we are! Although men may want it, and be happy to engage in it, too much contact too soon spooks them. He'll feel like he just got married in a blackout and want a quick emotional annulment! He hears the cage door slamming and will try to teach you both a lesson . . . that he didn't really mean it (yet). Unless you only want him as a lover, slow him down before you pull his zipper down.

Frequent Flyers
Is He Pathologically Incapable of Nesting, or Just Really, Really Busy?

Frequent Flyers are very hip to their dysfunction. Trust me. Any time I've dated one of these troublemakers, he breaks the bad news right up front. On a first date, he'll typically say: *"The last time I was in a se-*

rious relationship, my girlfriend threw a hammer at my head! I've been single ever since."

After you date him for a while, you'll want to hit him in the head with a hammer, too.

Clue: All his exes are nuts/psychos/stalkers! Of course, a Frequent Flyer would find someone he was justified in running away from, or he'd have to admit that *he's* the problem.

Now, commitment-phobes know that there's something wrong with them. The problem is, they're not usually willing to do anything to correct the problem, *or they'd be all better by now.* The real crazy-making part of this relationship will occur when you try to blow him off. Then he may start to fight for the relationship passionately.

MAN FACT: *The commitment-phobic man won't commit to stepping up, or breaking up. Breaking up would be a commitment, too!*

When confronted with losing you, he'll try to buy time, so that he can "figure things out."

WARNING: Unless he's figuring it out with a therapist, he's going to keep concluding that women suffocate him, and quickly bugger off again.

You'll probably be the one who calls it quits once you get clear about his chronic flight addiction. For the record, I think that true commitment phobia is rare. Usually the men who we thought were terrible flight risks weren't quite ready to settle down yet. They'll commit somewhere down the road, just not to us. Thank God, because that'll be ten years from now. By then, he'll be forty-five with the relationship skills of a fifteen-year-old and ready to work a relationship out with a twenty-two-year-old. I'm sure you'll be married with children by then, or having sex with strapping youngsters yourself, and will have forgotten all about him!

Is He a Flight Risk? Checklist

The do-it-at-home checklist for commitment phobia.	YES	NO
Can't step up	—	—
Can't break up	—	—
Can't say the word we	—	—
Tenses when touched in public	—	—
Introduces you as his "friend"	—	—
Pretends he's allergic to your cats	—	—
Refers to his divorce as the happiest day of his life	—	—
Doesn't own pets	—	—
If he has plants and they're still living, he has a gardener	—	—
Made plans to spend Christmas without you	—	—

Buys you a T-shirt for Valentine's day	—	—
Doesn't go on vacations with you	—	—
Has girlfriend replacement gadgets, like massage chairs, personal assistants, chefs, and maids	—	—

Tip: If you've checked yes to three or more questions, buy handcuffs.

The F.U. Gitive
(aka Vagrant Migration)

The F.U. Gitive is like *The Terminator*.* His hostility just keeps re-booting. His behavior is deeply passive-aggressive and is definitely meant to hurt you. He's the bastard who stands you up for Christmas at your parents' house, leaves you standing at the altar, or picks a fight the day before you're planning to go on vacation and flies the coop without you.

The F.U. Gitive is manipulative. He picks an irrational fight to distract you from whatever plot he's hatching. This *decoy fight* is designed to keep you spinning and to distract you from whatever betrayal he's really planning (like sleeping with a bridesmaid in the cloakroom before your sister's wedding). Then, unbelievably, he'll excuse his behavior by blaming it on you. *"Well, if you hadn't been such a bitch, I wouldn't have had to sleep with her in the first place! I've decided to only sleep with women who act like they* like *me."*

This tactic is designed to make him feel better about pulling the romantic rug out from under you. But he won't really feel bad about it one way or the other. After all, he's not the one getting screwed over, *you* are. F.U. Gitives are dangerous predators who tear off into a sky full of gathering cumulous clouds and ominous thunder. A very heavy rain is sure to follow (your tears!).

---

*The original, not the sequel

If a man exhibits this kind of dastardly behavior more than once, put him in total isolation for life with no chance of parole. He is damaged goods and a hardened romantic criminal. Drop him from the flock and quickly put his head on the chopping block.

MANHANDLING MANEUVER: *Stop hoping and start hating! Sometimes hate can be healing, too.*

twenty-one
The Male Secret Language Decoder

The following birdcalls are typical of the easily startled modern male. Whether you've been with him for two weeks, two months, or two years, use this decoder to translate what he's actually saying when he utters the following phrases.

"I'll call you . . . tomorrow." *Translation:* "I want to get off the phone now."

"I'll call you soon." *Translation:* Unfortunately, we have no way of determining the meaning of this with today's current technology.

"I'm fine." *Translation:* "Please shut up or change the subject."

"No problem." *Translation:* "I heard you. You can stop talking now."

"No, really, that looks great on you!" *Translation:* "If I tell you the truth, you won't blow me tonight."

"I'll help you in a minute." *Translation:* "Go ahead and do it yourself."

"I'll call you." *Translation:* "I'm not calling you until I start lusting after livestock."

"I need some space." *Translator's Note:* Meaning is completely dependent upon how totally you've managed to piss him off. *Translation:* (1) "I want to temporarily break up with you and have sex with my secretary." (2) "Back off! You're pressuring me and I'm teaching you a lesson." (3) "We're breaking up."

"I feel trapped." *Translation:* "Get off my back, woman!"

"I need space, I feel trapped." *Translation:* "We are breaking up right now. And don't forget to take your Tampax with you."

"I love you, but I'm not in love with you." *Translation:* "I'll sleep with you, but you've been demoted to booty-call status."

"I'm not looking for a relationship." *Translation:* "I'm not looking for a relationship with *you.* But we can have sex together until I find someone I decide to fall in love with."

"I'm enjoying my freedom right now." *Translation:* "I just dumped my girlfriend and I'm having the time of my life. But I'll be happy to put you into romantic rotation for a little workout!"

"I don't want to get married." *Translation:* "I don't want to get married to *you.* But I'll be happy to date you until you start bringing up marriage, and then I'll remind you that we had this conversation and I won't feel guilty because it's your fault you didn't believe me when I told you I didn't want to get married to you, you nagging bitch!" (*See* Secret Male Lemon Law Disclaimer, page 63.)

"I don't want children." *Translation:* "Whoa, slow down, are you kidding? I don't even own plants!"

"It's not you, it's me." *Translation:* "It's definitely *you*, trust me. I just don't want to go through the aggravation of discussing it and getting you even more pissed off at me."

"It's not me, it's you." *Translation:* "It's definitely *me*, but I'll try to keep the audition process going as long as possible until you get wise and finally dump me."

"Let's hang out." *Translator's Note:* Has a variety of meanings: (1) "Let's go out and see what happens. I really like you." (2) "You're a booty-call." (3) "I'm not sure if I'm really attracted to you, so let's hang out and see what happens."

"Let's hook up." *Translation:* "Don't expect too much, 'cause I'm too cheap or too blasé about you to bother spending money on you. But we can definitely have sex if you want to!"

"I like you as 'a friend.'" *Translation:* "I definitely don't want to have sex with you (right now)."

"Later, dude." *Translation:* "I do not, will not, and cannot think about you in a sexual way. EVER."

"I love you." *Translator's Note:* Correctly interpreting the meaning of this phrase is completely event dependent:

DURING SEX: "I love having sex with you."

DURING A FIGHT: "I'm trying to distract you from the fact that I slept with your best friend."

FIRST THING IN THE MORNING: "Seriously, I really, really love you."

"OH CHRIST, I LOVE YOU!!": "Thanks for swallowing."

MAN FACT: *When you ask a man what he's thinking about and he says, "Nothing," he usually means it. Men, like Neanderthals, are often simply watching the fire and scratching their balls.*

Bizarre Birdcalls
Keeping (Phone) Tabs on Their Prey

Have you ever noticed that men seem to know exactly when you've stopped thinking about them and then, suddenly, they call? Your heart contracts. Or flips. Or stops. How did he know that you were almost free and then magically call you at that very moment?

I have discovered that men have an internal tracking system that allows them to calculate how long it will take for you to recover from whatever damage they've inflicted and crawl out of harm's way. Then they call you up to see if their talons (hooks) are still in. This is a genetic holdover from their cavemen days when their day job was hunting, wounding, and killing big furry bison.

Or they're psychic.

Nah! I'm gonna go with the Internal Prey Escape Meter.

You Haven't Heard a Peep

Dear God, let the phone ring.
It would be such a little, little thing ... just RING!!

–Dorothy Parker

He suddenly drops out of sight and you haven't heard a peep. There is nothing quite as maddening as waiting for a call from an errant lover on the wing. You go from anticipation to hope to worry to anger, and then manage to talk yourself back into hope all over again. You wonder if you should call him. Maybe he's ill, or in trouble ... *or maybe he got hit by a bus?!*

MAN FACT: *If a man isn't calling you, it means that he doesn't want to talk to you!*

At least not right now. But he'll call the second he pulls his head out of his ass. Wait him out. Back away from the phone and delete his number so you won't be tempted to call him on a whim. Trust me. Men always call again if they really care about you. Hopefully, you'll be happily dating a hot stud at the time and answer his call with a nonchalant "Hey, what's up, Brosif? Long time no speak."

Relationship guru Pat Allen says that you should accept the fact that a man has totally flown the coop if you haven't heard from him within two months. He's still a viable prospect if he calls within eight weeks, however, so don't fret! If there is a temporary communication blackout, he may be trying to wrap his head around the idea of stepping up and seriously dating you. So wait him out and give him his space.

MAN FACT: *If he's really falling for you, he'll call to "check in" within two months tops. Or right after he breaks up with his dental hygienist.*

The Come-and-Go Caller

Always beware the man who has sex with you and doesn't call the following day. He's distancing himself from you and the intimacy of the act, and he's sending you a very clear message: "Don't expect anything from me. I'm gonna try to get away with calling whenever I feel like it, and if you fall for it . . . why, that'd be perfect! I'd be delighted to have sex with you again."

So remember: After you've had sex, carefully observe his phone patterns for important phone clues of ongoing consistency, unless all you wanted was that sexy Jaybird's booty-call in the first place.

MANHANDLING MANEUVER: *When he finally calls, let his message go straight to hell* (voice mail). *Listen to his excuse, and then return it several (this means at least two) days later, if you so choose. He doesn't deserve any more enthusiasm from you than what he's so not showering you with. Respect thyself!*

ODD MAN FACT: *When you mirror a man's lack of interest, he'll often totally change his tune.*

When his distancing trick doesn't work the way it normally should (making you feel insecure so that you'll be overeager to rebook him), he may start to hunt you down. We teach men how to treat us, so educate him thusly: *"You seemed a little too blasé for me. I'd rather date in a nonsexual way for a while, George. Maybe we could get together and go bowling."* Any man willing to show up after hearing a line like this is worth giving a second chance to!

Out of the Clear Blue Sky
(aka the Wild Blue Yonder Caller)

It's been more than two months since he was on your radar and he calls you right out of the blue. What's a girl to do?

Options: If you choose to answer this call out of morbid curiosity, the tone to hit is one of friendly detachment: *"Well, hello, Howard, what's up?"*

Critical Tip: DO NOT FLIRT!

There are only five reasons why a man calls you out of the blue:

1. He's transitioning you from leading lady to a friend, and enough time has passed for this to occur.

2. He just cleared his romantic roster and wants romantic or sexual reengagement.

3. Plan A with an MVP fell through and he needs a date replacement.

4. He wants his leather jacket back.
Note to self: Make a trip to the Salvation Army.

5. He truly misses you and wants to take another shot at it.

Callback Rules for Out of the Wild Blue Yonder Callers

Stay Alert: Conduct this experiment in pristine conditions so as not to contaminate the results with a false positive. This may be the only (golden) opportunity to release yourself from the bondage of obsessing about this Nemesis Bird *for the rest of your life.*

1. Never ask him out.
2. Don't ask him where he's been.
3. Keep the conversation light and polite. Be upbeat and share great news, like your promotion or closing escrow on a new home. Let him know that your life is great. Remember, he is not a friend, he's your Nemesis Caller!

4. End the phone call first, and *if he asks you out, heads up:* It's a romantic do-over!

Fighting on the Phone

It is always unwise to fight with a man over the phone. There is no way to kiss and make up! If you're angry, let his call go straight to VM until you're calmer. You won't be put on the spot and will gain valuable time to regain your composure. Your temporary silence will speak volumes to a man. You are now speaking to him in his own language (space and timely withdrawal), and he will definitely get the message. Besides, recorded birdsongs yield tons of information, so listen carefully to his message for important clues . . . like an apology!

MANHANDLING MANEUVER: *Let your voice mail do the talking.*

Know When to Be Unavailable

Always screen the following:

A man who returns your call or e-mail three days to one week later. Attention: You are not a priority! He can't get nailed for being rude, but he is now contacting you in a way that is totally devoid of urgency.

ROMANTIC RULE: *Remember, if there is no urgency, then nature isn't calling him urgently, and that spells trouble for romance.*

The Late-Night Caller. Don't pick up after 10 P.M. unless he's taking you to Maui or has professed deep and abiding love for you. Otherwise, just screen him, and call him back during the light of day.

The Avoidance Caller. This crazymaker calls and leaves messages when he knows you won't be able to answer your phone, so that he can still get points for calling but manage to avoid speaking directly with you. What a clever bird! Take out your cleaver.

A man who demotes you from physical to analog to digital. A man who loves you will want to hear the sound of your voice, hold you in his arms, and see you in person. He won't be satisfied communicating with you via electronic media.

1. If a man lives in your neighborhood, he should call you on the phone and try to see you *in person.*

2. If he used to call you and starts e-mailing or two-waying instead, you're being *demoted.* This is a distancing technique and signals that he is stepping back without totally letting you go. You are now in romantic rotation. Position: benched.

3. Remember: If a man keeps it virtual, he's a virtual waste of your time. Don't allow phone calls, text messages, or e-mails to become "date replacements." Talk for five minutes tops and then hop off the phone first, by saying: "Well, it was so great hearing from you. Thanks for calling, but I've gotta run, hon." When men miss you, they'll make actual dates with you instead of settling for a chat. Warning: Men who want to keep it "virtual" are often cheating on their wives!

MANHANDLING MANEUVER: How to Virtually Knock Him Off His Perch

The e-mail romancer is the most likely to turn tail, so lower the boom and knock him off his perch quickly. E-mail him this way: "Dear Maxwell, I only regularly e-mail men who are out of the country, so please feel free to call me."

Then take him off your buddy list. He'll get the message.

ROMANTIC RULE: *Two-ways were meant to be in person!*

twenty-two

Has Your Relationship Gone to the Birds?

Stuffing the Bird

Most women love to fluff up everything around them. My calico cat was the recipient of much (unwanted) attention. He never asked to be put in a dolly dress, and in one photo is struggling with a cherry lolly that I rammed into his mouth "because he liked it." The bunny got sent to the vet when I "accidentally" hugged it too hard, and I broke my Easy-Bake Oven from excessive entertaining.

I, like so many women, needed to overcome the tendency to get carried away with the activities associated with being "in love." This is dangerous territory to tread on, especially in the courtship phase of a relationship. (Stick to bikini waxing, jogging, and dust busting.) Unfortunately, when you become a whirling dervish of romantic activity, you run the risk of stifling your suitor's natural instinct to ante up and build the relationship *with* you. Men are practical. If you're doing all of the hard labor, they'll take it as a cue to move their focus to other important things (like foosball), because in their minds . . . you're handled.

Don't give more time, energy, or attention to the men you're dating than they're giving back to you. Remember: Men fall in love through the process of doing. They need to build a nest around you to mark their territory and to make the relationship their own. If you're always one step ahead of them, they'll feel unappreciated, unnecessary, and even emasculated. This dynamic will not result in the torrid sex that you deserve!

ROMANTIC RULE: *Overgiving short-circuits the male coupling instinct! If your man has become romantically lazy, it's probably because your overabundant giving has drowned his desire to win and woo.*

When you're stuck in quicksand, the more you do, the deeper you'll sink. At this juncture many women sink even deeper by mistakenly thinking that they're not doing enough to please their man. In a panic, they redouble their winsome efforts in a misguided attempt to revive his ardor and attention.

The only way to get unstuck is to stop acting like Santa in a mini. When he finally calls you again (and trust me, they almost *always* call again), let him take *you* out to dinner, let *him* pick up the check, and let him give *you* head. The only thing you're allowed to do is enjoy yourself, and the only things you're allowed to say are "A little to the left," "Yes, right there!" and "Thank you!"

Overgiving creates guilt, not marriage. Most men believe in the scales of justice and don't want to be characterized as being selfish or unfair. The biggest reason *not* to overgive is because it makes your man feel guilty. He'll only wind up feeling manipulated by racking up a romantic debt that's not of his own making.

MAN FACT: *Men are professionals at keeping score!*

Most men secretly enjoy jumping through hoops of fire, scaling craggy cliffs, and bringing over Chinese takeout. But if you tip the scales of romantic justice and burden a man with a love debt, it will ultimately backfire. Usually, the trouble begins when you notice that he's not really reciprocating in kind.

Many women will now start to make the classic mistake of complaining about everything they've been doing for *him*. Who asked you to teach his children French anyway? (You!) This is a terrible way to get your man to make a deeper commitment, and you risk violating the supreme rule of male courtship: *Men only do what they want to do.*

No matter what men say, watch what they do. When we stuff the bird, men construe it as pressure, and a big reaction is sure to follow. Overgiving can induce La-Z-Boy Recliner Syndrome or turn your Lovebird into a Bat Out of Hell. If the gods really want to punish you for poor manhandling, you might even wind up with six feet of trouble. He's the type who'd be more than happy to sit in your nest and channel surf until you come home from a hard day at the office, and expect you to cook him dinner.

Instead, when you wisely pull back, men will naturally pick up the slack and romantically reengage if they're remotely right for you. And you'll have given yourself the priceless gift of clarity. You might need to make some changes in how you choose to prioritize your relationship. Low self-esteem and fear of loss are usually the real reasons women start overcompensating in the first place. Don't despair! It will become easy to see what your partner's contributing to the relationship once you step back and stop overgiving. You'll be able to see exactly what you've got left on your plate, and then you can deal with the meal.

ROMANTIC RULE: *Slim Jims and Hershey's Kisses* do not *count as dinner.*

Circling Your Prey:
Help for the Chronically Obsessed

Do you obsessively think about "him" and "your relationship"? Learn how to snap yourself out of the hypnotic state you've put yourself into by "circling your prey."

ROMANTIC RULE: *No one is obsessed when their needs are getting met, unless they're lunatics.*

When a woman is tormented by love, she's usually hooked on a man who can't fulfill her most basic needs for love, attention, sex, intimacy, companionship, or commitment. In other words, you've either fallen in love with a sociopath . . . or a homosexual. If this sounds like you, the good news is that you're not wrong to feel bad, but the bad news is that once you've become obsessed, your relationship is usually bad news for you.

ROMANTIC RULE: *Being "in love" means that two people feel the same way about each other.*

In other words, if someone asked both partners how they felt about each other, they'd both say, *"I'm soooo in love!"* Otherwise, one of you is suffering from romantic delusions.

In other words, if you have to ask other people about what's happening in your relationship, you're not really in one. And if you can't talk to him about what's happening in your relationship, you don't have one.

The "Are You Obsessed?" Test

Take this test to determine the severity of your obsessive symptoms.

	YES	NO
Do you go to sleep thinking about him?	___	___
Do you wake up in the middle of the night thinking about him?	___	___
Do you wake up in the morning thinking about him?	___	___
Do you talk about him incessantly?	___	___
Do you make new friends so that you can talk about him some more?	___	___
Do you talk about him to total strangers and hairstylists?	___	___
Do you call the psychic hotline and talk to the dead about him?	___	___
Do you talk to spirits through tarot and the I Ching to divine his "inner thoughts"? (This actually works!)	___	___
Do you qualify to become a detective because of your covert sleuthing?	___	___
Do you Google him obsessively?	___	___
Do you frequently engage in hang-ups and drive-bys? (You're now officially stalking him, hon!)	___	___

If you answered "yes" to more than three, you're Officially Obsessed!

Obsessive Type #1: Breakup/Make-Up Obsession (Note: Not to be confused with actual Makeup Obsession with M.A.C. or Stila.)

Well, he dumped you. You weren't that into him during the courtship, but now all you want in the whole wide world is to *get him back*. You'll do anything because your bruised ego is pushing you beyond all reason. *Note:* This is not love, *it's personal!*

The uncertainty about when you'll actually see him is part of the allure of this relationship, and anxious tension supercharges each encounter with high drama. You feel like you're lovers reuniting after a war. You compulsively call him and persist in ridiculous, heart-wrenching conversations (Where did you meet that brunette? How old is she? Twenty-three?!). Finally, you'll resort to e-mailing, texting, and two-waying — and doing drive-bys in lingerie.

Symptoms: Engaging in lots of make-up sex and/or breakup sex

The Upside: Mascara streaks on cheeks give you a sexy punk-rock look!

Obsessive Type #2: Revenge Obsession: Tormenting Your Prey

Now you're having sex *at* him, not *with* him.

Fact: Revenge sex is often better than make-up sex, breakup sex, and even middle-of-the-night wake-up sex, but it's *very* bad manners! So only do it if you *really, really* want to.

Consequence: Total DRAMA!! This is only good if you're very bored and have no personal responsibilities, like work, pets, or plants; are independently wealthy; and know karate. Because he is going to absolutely want to kill you after you have sex with his business partner, brother, or best friend, or try to get him deported and put Nair in his shampoo. Revenge obsession is not only time-consuming, but also destabilizing and completely demoralizing. This is called "lowering the tone" and is not good etiquette. It has, however, been practiced by all the best families. (Think the Tudors, the Scotts, and the Medicis.)

Obsessive Type #3:
The Gone With the Wind Love Addict

You refuse to accept that this man does not, will not, or cannot ever return your affections. You stupidly pass up opportunities for true love because you're still carrying a torch for someone who has no real romantic interest in you. The torch that you're carrying is actually there to light the terrible darkness you're in. Girl, you're so stubborn, you must be a Taurus!

Problem: You are someone capable of mistaking friendship and sexual attraction with love.

Case Study:
Scarlett O'Hara, Love Addict

Scarlett O'Hara is the patron saint of all women living in obsession-driven denial. I interviewed her last spring, and although she's still not in recovery, I'm thrilled to report that she's taking great delight in tormenting all of the men at the Twelve Oaks Retirement Home.

ME: *So, Scarlett, what's become of your Captain Butler?*
SCARLETT: *That ancient history? I got over that silly crush! . . . Oh, and good morning to you, Morris! Don't you look handsome in your new blue cardigan. Why, yes, I'd be delighted to sit next to you at Bingo. . . . I'm sorry, what were you saying?*

ME: *Captain Butler? Are you still in touch?*

SCARLETT: *Well, I went to Charleston to surprise him that one time. But we're taking a little break right now. Did he ask about me?*

ME: *Um . . . Not exactly.*

SCARLETT: *Oh, let's talk about something else.* [Pause] *Oohhhh, look at that fat old India Wilkes. Isn't her dress just awful? I wouldn't be caught dead in it!*

Attention All Women Who Date Unavailable Men: Atlanta Is Burning!

If you've set your sights on an unavailable man, or worse, one who isn't even on the same page as you (you're stuck on page 22, but he's closed the book, or worse, thrown it at you!), here's a tip: T-H-E-R-A-P-Y. Consider it.

If you're not sure you're obsessed, call three of your closest friends and ask them if they think you're in danger of "being tragic" in the Victorian novel sense of the word, as in waiting-for-your-soldier-to-come-back-from-the-Civil-War kind of tragic.

Fashion Tip: This kind of drama only looks fantastic in a hoopskirt.

Unchecked, this kind of thing can go on for years. The good news is that you have a fabulous imagination! It will finally be put to excellent use if you decide to deprogram yourself.

Become a Member of the Mind Police

When you change your actions, your thoughts will automatically follow. The following seven steps are fabulous aids to help you release yourself from any obsessive spell.

1. Deprogram yourself. Delete his phone number from your cell phone, buddy lists, e-mail lists, and two-ways.

2. Change your habits. Instead of driving by his house after yoga, find an alternate route. *Tip:* It takes ninety days to break or create a new habit. Mark it on your calendar. Then have a cupcake!

3. Rubber band snapping. Put a large rubber band around your wrist and snap it *hard* every time you think about him. It will reveal how much energy you've been wasting on him and will soon become quite painful.

4. Recite the alphabet backward. This is very hard to do and will make it impossible to obsess about him — or anything else for that matter, so don't put on false eyelashes or operate heavy machinery when practicing this technique.

5. Visualize a STOP sign every time you think about him.

6. Practice aversion therapy visualizations. Imagine that he's got a *terrible* case of the crabs! And every time you long for his magic wand, imagine him reaching into his pants and scratching away like a dog with fleas.

And when all else fails, just try . . .

7. The Dick Replacement Program. Have sex with twenty-three-year-olds! This is fun, effective, the perfect way to get over the hump, and is *such* a boon for them.

twenty-three

Flipping the Bird

Surprisingly enough, most men polled suggested that instead of blowing them off, women should just blow them, although this, too, could lead to some very hard feelings!

–Dr. Lauren Frances, Ph. DD

Empty Nest Syndrome

You recently broke up and can't stand the loneliness. You're used to having a man in your bed. When a woman rushes back into the wilds, however, she may often wind up with some strange birds in her nest. This can send her even further into a slough of despondency (dating depression). What's a girl to do? This may be the perfect time to consider the recyclable male. . . .

Have Sex with an Ex

This is the magic doorway where ex-lovers can get back in. Sometimes it's not only the nice thing to do, it's the *right* thing to do!

Let's examine some of your options:

The Puddle Jumper. You call him and cry on his shoulder every time you break up. He spoons you, which is even more tragic than being alone because you just sort of lie there. He's the always-there guy, but for some reason you never take him seriously. He's so nice. . . . Too nice, in fact. *Hello!* Maybe you should up and marry him.

And then again, there's always Sven. Sometimes I find that having a lover named Sven really expedites my emotional healing. Although some may dismiss this as "hot rebound sex," it can really perk you up. When they're grieving, many of my patients have rebound sex, but often find it hard to keep the names straight.

Tip: I recommend calling everyone Daddy, Baby, Stud, Sir, or Loverboy.

Stick a Fork in It

Sometimes when women break up, they don't want to *stay* broken up (aka Relationship Recidivism). This is because most of us are true romantics and have an aversion to an unhappy ending. This state of affairs (sad!) often occurs when you won't close the book on a dead-end relationship and refuse to write THE END, because you don't like the way the story turned out.

Problem: Your hope is like watering leaves that have fallen off trees. You break up repeatedly, then get back together, then break up all over again, but never quite close the door on this relationship. If you're one of the many women who can't break off a dead-end love affair, I have one word for you: *closure.* Here's how to get it:

Stage a Relationship Funeral

Invite your Mantrap Pack and closest friends. You know, the ones whose shoulders are damp with your tears. The ones who are secretly

thrilled that you finally got rid of him so they can give up the suicide watch they've been on ever since your breakup.

Relationship Funeral Sample Script

As the scene opens, we pan in and see Marci's Mantrap Pack dressed completely in black. Candles are lit. Macabre techno music plays in the background.

ALISSA: *Dearly Beloved, we are gathered today to mourn the passing of Marci and Jonathan's relationship. There was a lot of great sex, hot dates, and verbal banter. And that trip to Guam. Didn't you get terrible food poisoning there, Marci?*

[MARCI nods.]

ALISSA: *That was probably a sign.*

GROUP: *Yep! Mmm hhhhmmm. Aha.*

ALISSA: *Unfortunately, this relationship was dead on arrival last April, but Marci kept it alive by tube feeding, selfless booty calling, intense prayer, and frequent drive-bys. Marci, would you like to say a few words?*

MARCI: *Well, yes, yes, I would. [Sniff.] Jonathan, as you all know, was a just a terrible skirt chaser. I totally deserve to be with someone who is truly available, steadily employed, and who wants to chase only one skirt . . . mine. But I did love him and will miss the way he used to talk in his sleep and played fetch with my cat. It was damned cute! [Hiccup.]*

ALISSA: *Thank you, Marci. Would anyone else like to say a few words?*

GROUP: *Remember when he got* ass *rash? Ewww!*

MANHANDLING MANEUVER: *You may also choose Bonfire Therapy as an alternative. Take significant mementos of your relationship, like vacation photos, concert ticket stubs, and his vintage Led Zeppelin T-shirt, and cremate them in your fireplace, or put them in a shoebox and bury it in the backyard. I'm a proponent of bonfire therapy myself, but that's just me.*

The Burial

Marci's Mantrap Pack helps her make a cardboard tombstone.

Jonathan & Marci

July 4, 1999, to June 28, 2006
Rest in peace*

THE END

---

* (or pestilence . . . it's up to you!)

Alissa leads the group in prayer:

> *"Ashes to ashes,*
> *Dust to dust.*
> *Now that you're free,*
> *A martini's a must!"*

And they quickly adjourn to a local bar to celebrate!

ROMANTIC RULE: *When you're having difficulty letting go of a relationship, stick a fork in it.*

Helpful Thoughts
When Your Goose Is Cooked

- If he were such a great guy, you'd still be with him.

- If he's making you feel this bad, he's not "the One."

- Their rejection is God's protection.

- You can't do the wrong thing in the right relationship. You can't do anything right in the wrong one.

- Your love counts even if your relationship didn't work out.

- Staying in resentment is like drinking poison and hoping that the other person dies.

- Poor me, poor me, pour me a drink!

twenty-four

The Pterodactyl

Are you getting hexed by your ex? If a ghost from your past is endangering your romantic future, it's time to do some spring cleaning . . .

The Pterodactyl is the extinct lover, "the one" who you're convinced was really "the One." *Problem:* He either dumped you or died, or you stupidly broke up with him for reasons that now, in hindsight, seem completely insane. And although you're no longer together (in this dimension), you can't quite manage to break up with him *in your mind.*

The Pterodactyl prevents us from being with living, giving, available men. Rather than risk another possible heartbreak, you've either stopped dating altogether or have become overly critical of new suitors. You see nothing but their faults and silently measure them against what could now be diagnosed as a Holy Grail–like obsession with how perfect "he" was.

In a truly honest moment, you'd probably admit that the only reason he seems so perfect is because he's not here. He can't leave his filthy gym socks on your white duvet cover or annoy you in the myriad of ways that real mortals do because he's engaged and has moved to France.

In fact, if you think *really* hard, you might even remember why you broke up with him in the first place. It was probably because he had some fatal deal-breaking flaw that you couldn't live with no matter how hard you tried.

Clues You're Living with a Pterodactyl

- You're still wearing his T-shirt to bed.

- When you spend quality time with your vibrator, his name comes up.

- The phrase "get back out there" makes you vomit in your mouth.

- You fear that close friends are screening your calls.

- You're wearing the engagement ring on your right hand or have craftily strung it on a chain around your neck.

- Or (this is serious) you're still wearing the diamond on your ring finger!

WARNING: Pterodactyls hang around because we haven't properly mourned their passing. They are common sightings in the lives of many lovely, lonely women. If your heart is obscured by a past relationship, swift action will need to be taken to walk you back into present time.*

Exorcising the Pterodactyl

He may be married to someone else, living upstate with a brood of five, or planted six feet under. Whatever his excuse, one thing's for certain: He's not here, and in all likelihood, won't be coming back to roost with you again in this incarnation.

---

* The biggest problem with Pterodactyls rattling around in your closet is that they're always getting tangled up in your Christian Louboutin shoes!

Attempting to exorcise the Pterodactyl unaided can be an arduous task. Many women are so plagued by repeat visitations that they're doubtful that they'll ever be free to love again. You may have even built up an entire mythology around him and keep paying psychic homage to a dead relationship as a way of keeping some thin connection alive. Like me, you've probably watched one too many episodes of *The Ghost and Mrs. Muir*. Please remember that Mrs. Muir *never* went out on dream dates, ever. If Mrs. Muir were here today, I'd tell her to use her first name and call a priest to exorcise her vacation home.

Tip: **Refrain from having long conversations with people who aren't actually in the room with you.** Buy garlic and crucifixes and stop chatting with sexy ghosts. Everyone knows that if you keep talking to them, they'll keep hanging about. Love phantoms are bored, and your attention is like irresistible French perfume.

(Remember, Blanche DuBois wound up in the nuthouse, even if she did get to make out with Marlon Brando in his prime.)

You will never be free of your Pterodactyl until you can accept the cold hard fact that *it's over*. Get out the white flag and surrender. There is no reason to give him any more of your valuable time and energy. If you don't, you'll never move on and wear that great garter belt that I know you've got tucked away in your panty drawer!

Go into mourning. Everyone looks great in black. Unleashing pent-up feelings will break your (dry) spell. Don't miss this opportunity to cry in restaurants and repeatedly send your food back.

Congratulations! If you've completed these operations, you'll be ready to UN-HEX YOUR HEART, so shut your door, light a candle, and pay close attention. We are now going to make a revulsion amulet to keep your seductive Romantic Vampire at bay . . .

The Amnesia List

To dispel unwanted "visitations," get a pen and make a list of *every single* irritating thing that you can remember about your Pterodactyl. Make sure to write down *everything*; from horrible character flaws (like when you met his ex and he "forgot" to introduce you) to bad habits (he liked to floss and talk). You can expand this list to include the pros and cons of the relationship, but in truth, you would probably be better served by a solid list of negatives. Here's an example:

Sample Amnesia List

- He could pronounce the word monogamy but had trouble defining it.

- Foreplay consisted of ripping the foil on the condom package.

- He wasn't at the airport to meet you after you flew ten hours to see him.

- The answer to any "relationship" question was two weeks of the silent treatment.

- He has a tattoo on his hip that says, TRUST NO ONE.

- He always wore socks, even if sometimes that's all he was wearing.

- He bought tires for your birthday.

- He thinks sneakers are shoes.

Keep this "revulsion amulet" with you at all times, no matter what. You can never tell when a love phantom will strike, so "better safe than sorry" as they say in France. It should fit nicely in your wallet or in the naughty nightstand drawer where you keep the condoms. And any time you find yourself humming his favorite song, or start to make out with him in your mind, whip out your Amnesia List instead, and read it all the way through. You'll remember all of the pain he caused you, and if all goes well, you'll be as appalled by his apparition as you would whilst bikini shopping underneath fluorescent lights at the mall.

Dismantling the Shrine

This is like taking down your own Berlin Wall to love. Put away all photos and significant mementos of "him," until you get over the hump and are dating again. Shoeboxes tucked away in dark corners are the perfect resting place for love-tainted mementos.

Don't wear the earrings he gave you for Christmas. Stop wearing his football jersey to bed. And *please* do away with that stuffed armadillo he brought back from that business trip to Texas.

But don't give away actual pets unless you don't like them, are allergic to them, or were only putting up with them because you were being a "good sport."

Starving the Pterodactyl

If he's still physically hanging around, or calling just to be "friendly" (to keep you on the string), or, even worse, sleeping with you once in a blue moon, you must cease all contact with him for at least six months. That means no phoning, e-mails, birthday cards, or faxes. If he doesn't respect your need for mental breakup space, add this to your Amnesia List.

Don't ask him to return your books, pillow, or wok. These are just lame excuses you've drummed up to stay in contact with him *and he knows it*. Don't try to rustle up any gossip about him or waste your time imagining what he's doing with . . . *her*. Instead, starve this ghost out of the landscape of your day-to-day mind and you'll make room for a brand-new love to fly in!

Pray for the Bastard

The final key to un-hexing your heart is to simply *pray for the bastard*. I don't know why this works, it just does. Try using this effective multipurpose prayer every day for two weeks, and just see what happens:

"Dear Lord, please let him get exactly what he deserves!"

This will free you from the negative feelings that keep you stuck in the past like psychic superglue. When you wish him well (a state of forgiveness), you free *yourself*, no matter how big a dick he was to you. This is exactly where you need to be (mentally) to find true love again.

Onward ho!

*Men are very naughty sometimes,
so don't take any crap!*

-Your Ph. DD

manhandling

part iii

Setting limits isn't rejection, it's correction!

twenty-five

Can You Train This Bird?

It is vital when you live with a pet that you learn how to train it. If your man struggles to maintain goodwill and good manners, he'll only cause you heartache! Always remember that the bird is the closest living thing to the *dinosaur*. Even in the happiest of relationships, your partner's ability to speak on command, maintain good indoor behavior, and be of good cheer when cooped up with you for extended periods of time will be limited at best. That's why every woman should have some manhandling techniques up her sleeve to make sure she doesn't get crapped on.

ROMANTIC RULE: *You shouldn't be afraid of your pets, wonder where they are, or have to guess if they love you, too.*

Men need to put a woman's happiness first because most women naturally care for others without any coaching whatsoever. It's hard-wired into our DNA. That's why men need to prove, through their actions, that they're willing to care about your happiness as much as their own. Your man will take cues from you about how you'd like to be treated, to see what kinds of behavior he can or cannot get away with. If you accept bad behavior and refuse to set limits with him, you'll encourage him to behave *badly*. To ensure that you don't saddle yourself with a selfish, unworkable, or obstinate man, you need to see if he cares enough about your relationship to take your coaching.

MAN FACT: *The Goddess already knows that you'll take care of him. We need to make sure that he'll delight in taking care of you.*

CPB: Cost Per Bird

Having a relationship shouldn't cost your peace of mind, self-respect, your family and friends who love you, or the special things that bring you joy. If you find that your CPB (cost per bird) is higher than your returns, the price you're paying is much too high.

Is He Teachable?

You won't know if you can effectively train a man until some kind of conflict arises. This "first fight" is a litmus test to evaluate your partnership potential. Conflicts are golden opportunities to find out a wealth of important information about your new friend. We want to see if he fights *fairly*.

ROMANTIC RULE: *This golden "first-fight" opportunity will present itself as a conflict of needs. It's like looking into a crystal ball and seeing your relationship's future.*

The way that a man communicates during a disagreement gives you a sneak preview of his problem-solving skills and, more important, it speaks volumes about his character. You want a man who not only cares about your feelings, but actually *enjoys* taking care of them. If you find yourself with such a man, you are in luck. You've landed a top-notch bird! His considerate behavior and responsiveness to your needs will build trust and a loving relationship. They are important clues that signal his capacity for successful pair bonding.

But if you find that your man's ego drives him to win at all costs, if he exhibits punishing behavior to make you submit to his will, or if he constantly flies into a rage, you've got trouble on your hands. Some men have never learned to coexist with a woman—or with another *human*, for that matter—and he's going to be a handful.

To Avoid Power Struggles

If your male exhibits Neanderthal-like behavior roughly 10 percent of the time, we consider this to be manageable boneheadedness. But if he acts like a knucklehead more than 15 percent of the time, you have a discipline and maintenance problem on your hands. If unacceptable dominance or aggression is exhibited, it should be corrected in a calm but firm manner immediately.

- Be firm without being dominating or punishing.
- Use effective manhandling tools.
- Respect your pet.

FYI: He should not feel that filling your needs is an imposition, or an impossible and unpleasant task. Men should accommodate reasonable requests at all times unless they're ill, or watching a ball game.

twenty-six

Birdshit

Nip Bad Behavior in the Bud

If you refuse to housebreak your pet, you'll wind up with a mess. *Don't be a moving target!* If your man continually exhibits aggressive or obnoxious behavior, ask yourself if it's something that you're willing to live with *for the rest of your life.* If you aren't, you must be willing to do what's necessary to remedy the situation. Then, with the patience of a saint and a backbone like Stalin's, decide on a course of action to retrain your bird. Consistency is key.

Manhandling requires self-discipline and self-sacrifice. If you want to train a man, you must be willing to retrain yourself, and change your own behavior *first.* Without self-discipline and introspection on your part, you'll never effect change in him.

WARNING: When you change your behavior, you should expect a man to be miffed about his loss of status. He may scream, become peckish, or fly the coop temporarily. Don't be cowed by his behavior but take comfort in the fact that once he's housebroken, he'll be so much more fun to live with.

Limit-Setting and the Modern Male

Men respond to actions, not words. They wrote the book on sweet talk, so they know instinctively that it's not what you *say*, it's what you *do* that counts. The most effective way to set boundaries with a man is to give him a time-out and take away privileges. In other words, real consequences for bad behavior.

Penalties are more effective than nagging and henpecking that he can easily tune out. If you're being treated disrespectfully, all of the conversation in the world won't change a man's rude behavior, but changing your actions certainly will! Let your behavior do the talking and show him exactly what naughty tricks won't be tolerated by you.

MAN FACT: *We teach people how to treat us. Men respond to actions, not words . . . unless you're talking dirty.*

Covering the Cage:
Boundary-Setting and Containment

Men who are emotionally healthy learn to contain themselves by taking a time-out when they're being hurtful to others. They take a break and then pop out of isolation once they've mastered their negative feelings.

Men who aren't self-aware don't know how to take a time-out and just terrorize everyone around them instead. This behavior is unacceptable and must be nipped in the bud. These men are tyrants and bullies. No amount of conversation with this little dictator will change his behavior one iota, but his fear of losing you may.

ROMANTIC RULE: *If his behavior is unacceptable, remove his favorite plaything . . . you!*

The best thing to do when men misbehave is to give them a time-out, like you would with naughty children. To do this you'll have to contain your feminine desire to caretake, overexplain, and overshare your negative thoughts or feelings with him. A woman believes that if she expresses feelings of hurt, vulnerability, or upset, a man will automatically understand and even hug her (like her girlfriends certainly would). This thinking is so misguided. When men are angry, their blood is up and their instinct to cockfight is aroused, and they often just get mad.

It is not acceptable to hit, scream at, or henpeck your bird. Excessive punishment will only cause him to put up a terrible fuss, and he may become quite provoked and display overt hostility toward you.

MAN FACT: *The best training for a bad bird is to cover his cage and abandon the field. Dignified withdrawal is by far the best route to harmony.*

When a man behaves badly, excuse yourself, and *stop talking*. Don't reengage until after he's settled down. You may even have to physically leave the room if he won't stop fighting. When you let go of the rope, he'll wind up on his ass, and hopefully it'll knock some sense back into him.

He'll soon notice that his rights have been diminished, and he'll be forced to accommodate your needs or accept the alternative without you having to scream or fight with him about it.

Give Him an Altitude Adjustment

Altitude, or being Top Bird, is the primary goal of most men. Their place in the pecking order at work and at home is of vital importance to them. Men naturally seek the highest perch in a relationship (dominance), while women are more inclined to take other people's needs into consideration (I must pick berries and burp the baby, too).

When men attain too high a vantage point in their quest to be Top Bird, they sometimes fall prey to the mistaken idea that their needs, wants, and desires should come first. A man may become cocky and selfish and start acting like a tyrant in the TV room. If you feel that your fella is taking you for granted, or is exhibiting aggressive or unpleasant behavior, quickly put him in his place by giving him an Altitude Adjustment.

MANHANDLING MANEUVER: *To train a naughty Parrot, instead of looking up at him on a branch above you, keep him situated so that his head is never higher than your heart. Take him down a notch! He needs to know that you're equals and that he won't remain king of the castle if he persists in foul behavior.*

Love Script
For example, if you're constantly making trips to his house, ask him if he'll come to yours. Say, *"I'm too tired tonight. Would you please come my way, Scruffy?"* If he says, *"No,"* (as we suspect he will) say, *"I'm disappointed but am going to stay home tonight. Sorry you don't want to join me. Guess I'll flip through my little black book and make a booty-call to my favorite Dodo."*

When your bird flies down from his perch and you're both seeing eye-to-eye once again, you may reward him as long as his behavior does not change accordingly.

ROMANTIC RULE: *Never put a man above your own heart.*

Does Your Man Have an Altitude Problem?

	YES	NO
The relationship is on his terms.	___	___
He makes unreasonable demands for your time and attention.	___	___
He treats you like a second-class citizen.	___	___
Most of the sacrifices in the relationship come from you.	___	___
He puts his needs consistently above your own.	___	___
He takes you and the relationship for granted.	___	___
He cops an attitude when you make reasonable requests of him.	___	___
He assumes that his point of view is always correct.	___	___
He is overly critical of you.	___	___
He tries to bully or intimidate and criticize you, alone or in public.	___	___
He makes fun of you, even though he says he's only "joking."	___	___
He exhibits hurtful behavior that he refuses to change.	___	___
He is uncooperative and refuses to assist you in normal ways.	___	___

If you've answered "yes" to more than one item, he needs to be taken down a notch immediately, hon!

MANHANDLING MANEUVER:

- Stop waiting on him hand and foot.
- Stop speaking to him if he is rude to you.
- Restrict sexual playtime.
- If he's taking you for granted, pull back and take good care of yourself first.
- He needs to be on his knees for a while, and not the other way around.*

* No blow jobs!

    If this fails, we'll move on to lion-taming techniques. For this you'll need: a chair and whip.

    Hmmm . . . maybe that's what he was after all along!

twenty-seven

Talk to the Animals

How to Talk to a Man
When He's "Having a Feeling"

It may be hard to believe, but men have feelings, too. Their "go-to" feelings are quite different from ours, however. Men are often uncomfortable with weepy, vulnerable feelings, so their favorite upset feelings tend toward one of two kinds of anger: actively hostile (martial) or passive-aggressive (glacial).

Symptoms of active Anger Mode (*macho*) include raging about, throwing fits, irritation, meanness, shouting, curtness, sarcasm, aggression, and/or fisticuffs.

Symptoms of passive-aggressive Anger Mode (*snotty*) include eye-rolling, face-making, withholding, silent treatment, pouting, groaning, sighing, disappearing, and/or sneaky plotting.

The best way to handle men when they're having a *feeling*, big or small, is to allow them to have it with minimal intervention. Step away when his feathers are ruffled and return once he's had time to settle down.

Often, you'll find that a man's "feelings" are triggered by the following:

Situational upset. Something happened to provoke a macho outburst of hostile feelings or bad behavior. It could be in response to an irritation with you, something at work, or a malfunctioning gizmo.

Male Attention Deficit Disorder, or M.A.D.D. It's a scientific fact: Men can only hear three sentences max before they start to tune you out. Anything over three sentences overloads them with too much information, causing men to panic, especially if the sentences are loaded with . . .

Heavy emotion (anger, tears, or both). This is liable to turn him into a Bat Out of Hell. He'll actively flee the scene of the emotional crime or go into an *Emotional Coma*. Strong emotions from you (*any*) actually cause him great alarm and trigger an inner defense system designed to shut him down, thus preventing and protecting him from an imminent threat (saying something stupid while you're crying and making things worse). When a man is in an Emotional Coma, he often becomes a Mute Swan and behaves as one temporarily incapable of speech. He, when pressed, may manage to grunt, *"I'm sorry,"* or *"It's not my fault!"* Leave this bird alone! When men become mute, you have said *enough*. Many women repeat themselves, mistaking his silence for actual deafness.

MAN FACT: *He heard you. His brain just needs time to catch up.*

Upside to Men Suddenly Struck Mute: Men often place themselves voluntarily in (emotional) lockdown by winging away, or falling mute, to stop themselves from bullying you or becoming overly aggressive.

Let him digest the information. In the meantime, get a manicure. When you return, see if he's figured out what you were trying to communicate before you left. If he pretends that nothing happened, try talking to him again without the waterworks, in three sentences max.

Let him respond or mull it over for a while now that he's heard you repeat it in a calmer tone.

Male (Emotional) A.D.D. and the Three-Sentence Rule

Scenario: You ask your man if you and he can "talk." About three sentences in, you notice that he's no longer talking or looking at you and, instead, has started playing a video game while nodding and grunting, "Uh-huh. Hmm-mm-hhm." You ask him to stop (whatever he's doing) and "talk" to you. He becomes ridiculously defensive that you've "accused him" of not paying attention and stalks out of the room.

Male A.D.D. usually occurs when a woman starts an unending stream of emotionally charged conversation (in Girlspeak, "sharing your feelings"; in Caveman, "nagging, bossing, and complaining").

Female *sharing* often produces feelings of anxiety and panic in men, who respond to it by swiftly repositioning themselves to create a psychic buffer. They will then proceed to tune us out by doing something more productive, like playing computer poker.

MAN FACT: *Grunting and physically remaining in a room with a woman who's talking at him is considered "communicating" by most men.*

This is not a strategy, it is a primal urge that even the most metrosexual man possesses deep in his genetic hardwiring. This tune-out is such an old, yet effective, coping mechanism that it's impossible to reprogram.

The Three-Strikes-You're-Out Rule

The most effective way to talk to a man about a "hot topic" is to ambush him. By using the three-sentence rule you'll slip right under his radar.

MAN FACT: *If you have to make a request of a man more than three times, you're not going to get what you need from him without a fight. At least not right now.*

You have struck out. Just accept it! Most women don't know about this rule and as a consequence, fall into the following trap:

Bungling the Three-Sentence Rule

Example: You're happily watching TV. Bob comes into the room, grabs the remote, and starts flipping the channels.

Sentence 1
JESSICA: *Bob, I would appreciate it if you didn't change the channel while I'm watching* Masterpiece Theater.

BOB: [Grunts.] *Umm-hmmm.* [Continues to channel surf.]

Sentence 2
JESSICA: *Bob, it makes me feel disrespected when I make a request and you completely roll right over me.*

BOB: [Silence, more channel surfing.] *What?*

Sentence 3
JESSICA: *Bob, would you please change the channel back?*
BOB: *Hang on.*

Sentence 4

JESSICA: *Hellooooooo, Bob? Earth to Bob! BOB! ARE YOU DEAF?*

BOB: *You are such a nag! Here, watch whatever you want!* [Tosses the remote control at Jessica and leaves the room in a huff.]

ROMANTIC RULE: *When you get what you want by nagging, you still lose. If you repeat something more than three times, you're henpecking!*

Correct Use of the Three-Sentence Rule

Sentence 1

JESSICA: *Bob, I would appreciate it if you didn't change the channel when I'm watching* **Masterpiece Theater.**

BOB: [Grunts.] *Umm-hmmm.* [Doesn't change the channel back.]

Sentence 2

JESSICA: *Bob, it makes me feel disrespected when I make a request and you just roll right over me.*

BOB: [Silence, more channel surfing.] *What?*

Sentence 3

JESSICA: *Bob, would you please change the channel back?*

Bob ignores her. Jessica walks out of the room.

MANHANDLING MANEUVERS:

1. Don't say anything else. Just get up and leave the room.
2. He'll figure out what he did, come after you, and apologize.
3. When he does, thank him for it, give him a kiss, and then enjoy your chick-flick programming.
4. If he doesn't respond, do something else until he comes and finds you.
5. Your absence will register and he will most likely apologize for being selfish.

When you make a request, don't fight about it. *Show* your man through your actions that you dislike his behavior and that you won't stick around for it. We have much better things to do with our time, like reading *In Style* magazine in the bathtub.

ROMANTIC RULE: *We don't compromise our dignity or become doormats when we use the three-sentence rule. It's one, two, three strikes, he's OUT.*

Conversing with the Emotional Bird

Always be a woman of few words when you need to discipline a man.

Example

JESSICA: *Bob, I don't want to go to the camping fiesta in the woods again this summer.*

BOB: *WHY NOT? I just bought a new pup tent and I swear it won't rain this year!*

JESSICA: *Bob, I just don't feel comfortable going. Thank you, but no.*

BOB: *Dammit! Why don't you want to go? Come on, don't be a spoilsport! What, you can't take a little rain, and mud?* [Slams fridge door, stomps around the room.]

JESSICA: *Bob, I don't want to fight about it. I just don't want to. Okay, I am going to take the dog for a walk now.*

Time to get out of Dodge.

When you come back, restate your concern: *"I'm sorry you're disappointed, but I really want to talk about going to Venice together, like we agreed we would last year."* When he complies, use the rewards system of man management and stroke him.

MANHANDLING MANEUVER: *Never prepare men for big talks. Just ambush them when they're in a pleasant mood and state your case in three sentences, tops. Don't get M.A.D.D., get even!*

"No" Is a Complete Sentence

If your man pushes you to do something you don't want to do, just say no. You don't have to explain it. Just claim it and state it. The less you say, the stronger your position will be. *Reason:* Women often feel guilty when they say no. We tend to overexplain why we can't do something in an effort to not hurt other people's feelings.

Men, however, will often use your explanation as ammunition and try to pick apart your case and break down your defenses by finding the loophole in your logic. This is what they do at work. And this strategy usually works on girlfriends.

So just say, "No!" and stand there. He will have absolutely nowhere to go. And then he'll ask, "Why not?"

YOU: *It's just my gut feeling. This is just not sitting right with me.*

Remember, *no one can ever tell you that your gut feeling is wrong.* Most people recognize that "the still small voice inside of you" is holy ground, often God-inspired, and most men are wise enough to stop arguing once this statement's been uttered. They'll back away from your hot topic and look at you as one possessed by spirits.

Boo!

Don't Corner a Man When His Feathers Are Ruffled

When a man is upset or irritated, it is only common sense to wait until he's smoothed out his feathers before trying to make him speak on command (i.e., engaging him in a "relationship talk"). If you persist in trying to make him perform this trick, you're only liable to hear some very unpleasant screeching, and your prodding will provoke aggression, pecking, sneering, or other hostile behavior.

If you cannot resist tempting fate, or if you have a pressing need that must be communicated, don't be surprised if he lashes out while you try to discuss things "reasonably" with him. Your poor timing won't seem reasonable to him (not right now, anyway). His feathers are ruffled, and any conversation (criticism) is too irritating for him to bear.

He needs to be put back in the cage for a relationship time-out, until he settles down.

The best way to defuse the situation is to say, "Hon, you seem upset right now. Why don't we take a break and talk about this later when you're calmer?"

MAN FACT: *When men are irritated, don't back them into a corner by making them speak on command, or they'll attack!*

How to Train a Screamer

No one deserves to be screamed at . . . not (even) men and most certainly not you! If you have a screamer on your hands, the bad news is that he's going to be a *total* pain, but the good news is that retraining him is a possibility, *if, and only if,* you use the following training routine religiously . . . and have very thick skin.

MANHANDLING MANEUVER: *You must commit to gaining the upper hand. You must set a boundary with him* every single time *that he starts to act up. If he won't take correction and pipe down, you must immediately leave the house, the restaurant, or the relationship, to teach this loudmouth that you won't put up with his negative behavior.*

Tip: Screamers are screamers because they like to scream. It works for them and *is an effective tactic that they use to make things go their way.* It's not your fault that he's screeching at you, so don't take it personally. *Never* engage in a screaming match unless you like yelling, too.

Shut Him Up or Shut Him Down

The following technique is taught in self-defense classes to thwart would-be attackers. Here's how to beat Old Yeller at his noisy game.

As soon as he starts to shout, put your hands up like Miss Diana Ross and say, "*STOP!*" once, and very firmly. This will stun him. He may act like he flew right into a plateglass window and stop dead in his tracks. He may even take a step or two back.

Then say, "You may not speak to me in that tone of voice." And stare him down.

If he pipes right up again, repeat the same gesture and give the next verbal command: *"Stop. Do not raise your voice to me!"* (Try practicing this process several times in the mirror or with girlfriends.)

If he refuses to knock it off and is unable to contain himself, say, *"You are too angry right now. We will talk when you are calmer."* Turn on your heel and then silently and swiftly leave the room.

If he screams down the hall after you, do not speak to him or reward this behavior by giving him any more of your precious attention. Quickly leave the scene. He has lost the privilege of communicating with you for the time being. Stick to it! Create a complete No Access Zone around you, which includes cell phones, two-ways, and e-mails, too.

Your Big Squawker will soon learn that you won't stand for his unacceptable behavior and he'll gradually knock it off because it fails to work on you. You'll successfully set a new standard of behavior for him and he'll be a keeper, not a screecher.

WARNING: If you are inconsistent with this training, he won't believe you or respect you, and the next time you try it, he'll remain an incorrigible loudmouth.

You deserve better. So stick to it. You're worth it.

MANHANDLING MANEUVER: *Don't stick around for bad behavior. Quickly Cover the Cage and give him a time-out.*

Feather-Picking (on You)

This bad habit is caused by boredom and pent-up energy. If your naughty bird starts picking on you, quickly nip it in the bud. Never, ever allow a man to ridicule you. To shut him up, say, *"You're entitled to your opinion, but I don't have to listen to it. It's hurtful."* Then Cover the Cage by leaving the room or hanging up the phone . . . and then why not pull out your little black book and take a look? Or take up boxing and start practicing a great left hook!

Magic Words: Guaranteed to End Any Argument with Any Man

If you've tried everything else and nothing seems to work, you can always resort to magic. The following words are to be used only in a last-ditch effort to save your sanity. They are guaranteed to make a Trumpeter Swan as quiet as a House Wren.

Reciting these spells will allow for a little relationship cool-down period and give you the upper hand. In the heat of any argument, simply say, *"You might be right, Dwight,"* or *"All right, Zack, let me think about that!"*

Don't say anything more. Let him sputter around for a minute and wind down. You may have to repeat these sentences several times to reassure him that the fight is really over (for now) to complete his transformation from noisy and peckish to refreshingly mute.

But if he still won't pipe down, try, "Would a blow job make you shut your trap?" and I guarantee that he'll pipe down in two seconds flat!

twenty-eight

Peckerheads

Healthy men find it natural to want to make women happy. They protect and care for females, children, and society at large, instinctively. These noble birds don't worry too much about themselves because they know that when they provide care for others, their needs will be automatically taken care of, too.

So, when Average Joes ante up, they begin to possess a measure of greatness, enough to become heroic in the bedroom, in the boardroom, or on the battlefield. And we salute them! Because your happiness is the key to his sense of self-esteem, your ongoing love, trust, and respect will surely be his reward.

(Unless you're psycho.)

Then there are Peckerheads. These men are more like large boys zipped into man-suits. The Peckerhead is selfish, self-involved, and under the mistaken impression that women, relationships, and the entire world at large are simply there for his pleasure. He will deforest a nature preserve and quickly strip-mine your heart. He is conscience-free and won't adapt his hurtful or selfish behavior to accommodate your needs. Why should he? Your happiness doesn't come first. *His does!* No matter how charming he appears to be at first glance, you'll soon learn that the pecking order of this relationship puts your needs at the bottom, and his right on top, where, I might add, he can take perfect aim!

ROMANTIC RULE: *How you and your partner deal with troubles, trials, and tribulations will be a source of renewed camaraderie and understanding or divisive and destructive battling. So choose well, my lady.*

When His Feathers Are Ruffled: How to Spot the Problem Bird

You wouldn't want to handle an angry or aggressive bird without putting protective gear on first. Ergo, when a man is angry or upset, it's always wise to handle him with kid gloves.

Now, if your bird is chronically upset, irritable, and angry, it begs the obvious question of what in God's name you're still doing with him. Life's too short to be tyrannized by a badly behaved man. You must be able to retrain him. If he cannot be easily domesticated, quickly release him back into the wild before he destroys your peace of mind (or your furniture).

Most often, when men are upset, they take off in various Flight Patterns, as we've previously discussed. They flee your presence and then alight on your perch once they're delightfully human again. Other males, however, don't leave the cage, and will actually bar the door and fight it out with you. This occurs when a conflict triggers his *Fight Pattern*. In this case, men draw their swords and are willing to duel. A sparring match with an angry Raptor is unpleasant. He's lost all sight of you and has gone into battle mode and is rattling his rusty sword.

Warring Signs

He may start picking on you, taunting you, or even become meaner when you start to cry. When men do this, you must put them into total isolation because the man you love has just morphed into a . . .

Peckerhead. This condition occurs when your tears make him feel manipulated and he actually becomes meaner if he's made you cry. Or he's feeling guilty about something and won't cop to his bad behavior, so he'll start a fight to alleviate his guilt and make himself feel better. This is a terrible state of affairs and should not be allowed to continue. It should be a temporary condition and exhibited on rare occasions. If this happens more than twice a year, you have misdiagnosed this condition. You have confused the garden-variety Peckerhead with a . . .

Toxic Peckerhead. This man just likes to fight. Men who like to fight do it to find relief from their own crappy and stressful feelings. Toxic Peckerheads pick fights with valet parking attendants, ticket takers, total strangers, and their girlfriends. This is their version of stress management. Toxic Peckerheads are incapable of blissful domestication or loving pair bonding. They repeatedly betray your goodwill and your relationship by recurrent screaming, nipping, and nit-picking. They'll often blame their bad behavior on you. *Don't fall for it!* This bad bird is a big bully and wants a (smaller) sparring partner to use as an emotional punching bag for his do-it-at-home anger-management workout.

Early warning signs: He has road rage. He often yells when he reenacts hostile confrontations that he's had with someone else, and often while you're both stuck in the car. The tip-off to his aggressive behavior may come early in your relationship, but you may disregard it because it has nothing to do with you (yet!). But soon, you'll see it directed at you.

Question: *Do you really want to climb into the cockfighting ring? Will your manicure survive?*

WARNING: If you're trying to housebreak a Toxic Peckerhead, don't do it alone. Call a therapist for an intervention.

Or bring home an alleycat!

Does He Turn a Deaf Ear to a Distress Call?

I was at a cocktail party one night when I spied some interesting relationship behavior between Maggie, a brilliant colleague of mine, and her husband, Jimmy. He would peer around a corner, spot Maggie, and then give her a thumbs-up sign, and once she returned it, dash off again.

"Maggie," I asked, "what's up with Jimmy? He's acting kind of funny."

"Oh, the last time we went to a party he ignored me all night, and when I told him about it, it must've made an impression. He's just making sure I'm all right." She giggled. "I love that Jimmy!"

Observation: Maggie told her husband how she felt; Jimmy listened to her sadness and came up with an adorable solution. Getting her needs met by Jimmy is easy because he is not a *lunatic*.

But what happens if you're with someone who responds like Clark?

The Switcheroo

"Clark, it really bothered me when you left me alone at the party last night. I felt kind of left out. You didn't seem to notice that you weren't including me in conversation."

"Jesus, will you get off my back? Why are you so sensitive/needy/ clingy/insecure?!"

Clark just turned your valid need into an *insult*. He's a Peckerhead!

Or how about Matt?

The Swoop and Kill
"Matt, it really bothered me when you left me alone at the party last night."

"Fine. Next time I'll just go by myself if you hate my friends so much!"

Matt dismissed your need entirely and trumped it with a threat or punishment. He's a big bully!

And what happens when we discuss our tender feelings with Jack?

Big Baby with a Broken Wing
"Jack, it really upset me when you left me alone at the party last night. Your weird friend kept hitting on me."

"Would you stop busting my balls? I have a horrible headache. All you ever do is complain. I can't do anything right! Where's the Advil?"

Jack avoids the issue and acts like the victim, instead. He's a manipulative baby!

Men who think you're busting their balls when you make sincere requests are out of order. They are defending their right to be unworkable and unchangeable. Women are very susceptible to big babies because we hate to think we're hurting *anyone*, even men who are hurting us.

MAN FACT: *Men need to take your coaching without acting like they're getting their balls busted.*

The Fighting Cock

Fighting Cocks are dangerous birds of the wild. It may be disastrous to remove them from their natural habitats (inner rings of Hades) to try and tame them.

The Fighting Cock is also known as the I'm-Not-Going-to-Jump-Through-Hoops-for-You Guy. He is so insecure that even asking him to *consider* your feelings will be perceived as an affront to his masculinity. He'll quickly dig in his heels and obstinately refuse to cooperate for pleasant indoor living.

Fighting Cocks suffer from Little Dick Syndrome and try to boost their low self-esteem by fighting with women (and total strangers). Your needs are a perfect place for the assault because it's where you're already feeling vulnerable. Once you make a request, no matter how small or heartfelt, a Fighting Cock will throw down the gauntlet and refuse to cooperate with you as a personal point of honor. He childishly behaves like it's beneath his dignity to care about your feelings or to change his behavior for you in the slightest. He doesn't care about making you happy. He hates himself so much that he wants you to be unhappy, too. His is a dangerous kingdom, ruled by a crazy king.

Thank God he doesn't have a guillotine!

ROMANTIC RULE: *Don't try to partner with men who are chronically oppositional and refuse to compromise. Even if they're celebrities!*

The Fighting Cock thinks women are there to please *him*, no matter how badly he treats *them*.

If you have this foul fowl on your hands, get out the chopping block, preheat oven to 350 degrees, and make a tasty dead duck l'orange!

MAN FACT: *Hygiene issues are correctible with a good bar of soap, but a poor character is not so easily remedied!*

How to Spot the Difference Between a Noble Bird and Peckerhead

If he . . .

- is a graceful loser

- respects your boundaries

- recovers quickly from discord

- doesn't carry a grudge

- fights fair

- compromises

- takes responsibility for his part

  He's a Noble Bird!

But if . . .

- he blames you, refuses to apologize, and punishes you

- his inner sense of self-worth depends on winning every argument

- he turns on you or tries to bully you

He's a Peckerhead!

What, Do I Have to Act Like a Saint?

By now, you may have realized that it will take the patience of a saint to handle the little crappers. When you're at your wits' end, try the Saint Francis prayer. He is the patron saint of all women desperately trying not to break several clauses listed in the Ten Commandments when dealing with the most maddening of all of God's creatures next to horseflies, men.

Saint Francis was also famous for three things:

1. He meditated for hours in the woods.
2. He meditated for hours in the woods, nude.
3. He was so relaxed that birds actually perched on him.

He is often pictured with several birds sitting on his head, shoulder, and lap.

Whenever you need an attitude adjustment of your own, shut the door, grab a magazine, lock the door, and give Saint Francis a shot before committing relationship homicide.

Or you can try this shorthand version:

"God, please don't let me fricassee my boyfriend!"

Chapter Wrap-up

Everyone has idiosyncrasies and quirks. They're a part of the eccentric charm of being you. You need a man who doesn't think that you're too much work . . . for him. And vice versa. The right guy will turn your fear of bats into an opportunity for him to show his love by escorting you safely out of a dark, smelly bat-ridden cave.

Translation: Your hero!

twenty-nine

Putting All Your Eggs in One Basket

Most men will delay moving the relationship forward, even if they're madly in love with you, because they innately fear emotional lockdown. Unless you're dealing with a Homing Pigeon, you'll have to remind them when the expiration date on their exclusivity freebie is up. If, as the date approaches, your bird still hasn't said a peep about it, you should alert him thusly: *"Jackson, we've been dating for almost one year. I won't feel comfortable continuing our relationship without an engagement, as we have discussed before."*

Then *stop talking* and hear him out. If he has a wonderful surprise for you, *magnifique!!* But if your boyfriend is like most men, he'll just try to duck the question to buy himself more time, test your resolve, and try to maintain the status quo. This is your cue to put on your badge and lay down the law: say, *"I love you babe, but if you don't want to move forward, I will need to move on."*

Now watch, wait, and listen . . .

At this juncture, most birds usually start singing a very long list of excuses to prevent their permanent capture. Don't become alarmed if they pitch a fit, pick weird fights, become cold and withdrawn, or even threaten to end the relationship. He'll try very hard to regain control, and do everything in his power to make you extend the deadline, and duck your request, by terrorizing you.

The Duck and Cover

The art of avoidance, evasion, and lying (by omission) is a basic survival tactic that your Lovebird will exhibit to greater or lesser degrees when confronted with the prospect of having "the talk." This tactic is the hands-down favorite go-to strategy that men use anytime a hot topic comes up that they don't want to discuss. Men employ the art of avoidance to ensure that your agenda won't ever come up for discussion!

MAN FACT: *Conversations about important topics are commitments!*

If you have "the talk," he'll be forced to take a stand. Otherwise, a man continues to reap the benefits of all the "free stuff" he's been getting without having to make a deeper commitment.

Let's take a look at how men masterfully resist emotional arrest by keeping your relationship in a holding pattern, so they can stay Top Bird and keep calling the shots.

Tactic 1: Avoidance

AVOIDANCE *n* 1. deliberately avoiding; keeping away from or preventing from happening. 2. "Babe, I'm already late for work . . . can we talk about this later? Gotta run!"

Avoidance by stalling and delaying the danger. You: *"Where is this relationship going? When can we talk about getting married?"* Him: *"Can we talk about this later? I can't even think about that right now. I have to [finish my dissertation, get a promotion, buy a house, get my ex to sign the divorce papers, pay off my student loan, win that trip to the Caribbean, climb Mount Kilimanjaro] before I can even think about being ready to discuss that! Okay? Will you pass me the chips?"*

Avoidance by feigning illness. He may suddenly get a headache, backache, or some other impossible-to-prove he's-just-faking-it-to-avoid-having-a-serious-conversation type of ailment: "I have a really bad headache right now. Can we talk about this later? Would you rub my back a sec . . . ahhh, that feels so good!"

Avoidance by flying out of the room. He manages to disappear right in the middle of the conversation. He may wander out of the room, start another activity, or suddenly remember he needs to go to work, run an errand, or return to his apartment, thus masterfully managing to escape having "the talk."

Tactic 2: Evasion

EVASION *n* 1. a statement that isn't literally false but that cleverly avoids an unpleasant truth. 2. the act of physically escaping from something (an opponent or a pursuer or an unpleasant situation) by some adroit maneuver. "Hey, hon, I'm gonna make a beer run. Back in a few!"

MAN FACT: *Men know that withdrawing their attention drives women crazy. Your bird may actively choose to pull his attention away to punish you for trying to have "the talk," to get you right where he wants you—on the branch below him, and out of your tree!*

Evasion Technique 1: Dive Bombing

You start to have "the talk," but he changes the subject by bullying you. He gets really mean, upset, or grumpy to throw you off balance and scare you out of having "the talk." "You have such crappy timing! If you need an answer right now, the answer is no! Why do you always do this? Can't we just have a good time? This is the last time I ever take you on vacation. Jesus!"

Evasion Technique 2: The Boomerang

He derails the conversation by talking about some beef that he has with you instead. He plays a verbal shell game called "the Boomerang." It's very easy to get knocked off balance by this maneuver until you understand it. This is how it works.

YOU: *Moe, I've been patient, but now that your divorce is finalized, I'd like to discuss when we are going to get married.*

MOE: *You have got to be kidding me. I'm still steamed about what happened yesterday at the barbecue. Why did you wear such a low-cut blouse to my mother's house?*

Love Script
Respond with, *"You're changing the subject. We can discuss my wardrobe, but not until you answer my question."*
Then restate your topic again. See if it gets any traction . . . or if it goes straight to hell in a handbasket like this . . .

Evasion Technique 3: The Somersault Assault

YOU: *Moe, it's been four years now and I've been really patient. You said we would discuss this after your divorce was finalized, and it is.*

MOE: *If you aren't happy with the way things are right now, then why should I marry you? I don't want to be with someone who's unhappy.*

YOU: *Well, I am happy, but I'm not happy with the status of our relationship, especially after we came up with a date together . . . and that date has come and gone.*

MOE: *Well, I obviously can't make you happy, so let's not discuss marriage. Happiness should build on happiness. I'm not going to jump through hoops trying to please someone who can't be happy right now!*

He is doing more flips than Bruce Lee in an attempt to keep you spinning and knock you off balance. If you're engaged in a conversation with a man who tries this maneuver, the only thing to do is to stand up for yourself. Be prepared to walk . . . or submit to his terms and kiss his ring. (*See* case study *The Godfather.*)

WARNING: Savvy Romantic Researchers don't fall for avoidance routines, even when his excuses sound plausible. You have him on the run! When men start exhibiting avoidance behavior (flying around in a panic), it's actually a very good sign. Enjoy their flighty display! They're taking you seriously. They now know that you're no longer willing to wing it or allow yourself to fall into the trap of No-Time-Frame Dating. You both previously agreed on a time frame, and now they'll need to honor it in order to keep you.

So always remember . . .

If he says that the "timing just isn't right" or that your relationship isn't "perfect enough yet," remember that marriage vows are "For better or for worse," not "For better and completely perfect."

ROMANTIC RULE: *The right time to move things forward is when two people simply do it. Period. It's not brain surgery, here, people.*

Let's do an assessment of your fieldwork and examine what's wound up in your nest.

Does Your Relationship Add Up?

Once you learn a bit of relationship math, you can save yourself years of heartache—and its ultimate result: division! Use this romantic calculus to quickly predict your relationship's probable outcome.

Romantic Equation 1 + 1 = 1

Two incomplete and wounded people cling to one another in an attempt to make one whole person. This is the "you and me against the world, babe" relationship, which is codependent in nature. One or both partners are usually in "active" addiction or have poor boundaries from growing up in a dysfunctional family. The hallmark of this relationship is that one or both partners feel like they've taken on too much responsibility for the well-being of the other, almost as if they've been taken hostage. This is an unhealthy and immature relationship paradigm.

Relationship Calculation = You're LOON(atics)

Romantic Equation 1 + 1 = 2

Two individuals are complete in and of themselves, but they don't know how to compromise, surrender, or sacrifice their personal agendas for the good of the relationship. One or the both of them acts like the relationship is there only to serve them, and this selfishness will be their undoing. Partners fight tooth and nail to get their way and don't see the real damage they're inflicting on their mate. The hallmark of this relationship is intense power struggles and ceaseless fighting. This couple's inability to compromise and problem-solve will eventually undermine any peace or happiness they once had. They may leave the relationship as bitter enemies.

Relationship Calculation = The COCKFIGHTING DUO

Relationship Equation 1 + 1 = 3

This is the ideal partnership equation. You are separate but whole individuals, and you've come together to form a third entity: your relationship. You learn how to balance your individual needs with the needs of the relationship. You know how to problem-solve with each other respectfully and fairly. You are in a mutually responsible and loving partnership that can span the ages of time.

Relationship Calculation = You're LOVEBIRDS!

thirty

Swan Songs

Delivering the Timely Ultimatum

The follwing maneuver should only be used if you're committed to your personal relationship goals enough to move on.

How to Get a Man to Step Up or Step Off

Step 1. Cock the Gun

WARNING: Speak these words only if you're prepared to walk away and possibly never see him again. Or wind up married to him!

Love Script
YOU: *I can't stay in this relationship if we can't move forward to-gether and make plans for the future. I love you, but I am leaving you. If you ever want the things that I want, I am sure you will let me know. But until then, this relationship is over.*

HIM: (Gulp.) *Whaaaa?*

Step 2. Kick Him Out of the Nest

Immediately break up with him! If you're living together, pack your bags and rent a U-Haul. (Tip: Ask sexy men friends to help you move your furniture!) Remember, when you step back, you'll give him room to step up—or step off and stop wasting your time! You deserve a man who loves you enough to honor his word and keep his commitments.

Step 3. Create a Psychic "No-Fly Zone"

If your man stubbornly insists on behaving like a chicken, and stupidly lets you leave him, he may suddenly "come to" and try to woo you back with wheelbarrows of flowers, frantic phone calls, and desperate text messages—or the surprise 3 A.M. tearful drive-by.

WARNING: Don't become flustered and just cave in! He's counting on this kind of over-the-top wooing to get you back in line. Don't see him unless you're sure he means business. Here's how to flush out the truth of his intentions.

Love Script

"*I love you and am sad that you don't want to* [get engaged, have a baby, marry me, move in together, buy a home, have a future with me]. *I accept your decision. This is very hard for me, so please don't contact me for three months. I'll need some space and the room to move on. Bye, baby.*" Now completely stop talking and listen! If he has changed his tune, and says he's ready to step up . . . wunderbar! But if he's still flapping around, he was just testing you. This love script will let him know that you mean business.

Then get off the phone and stick to your guns! Give him a real time-out, because he actually needs one.

He needs time to carefully weigh his options. Does he want to have (a) sex with a slutty stranger in an elevator, or (b) a family, home, children, pets and plants, and someone who'll give a crap when he has a heart attack?

Step 4. The Standoff

Men at this point may either fall silent and withdraw, or fight it out to get you to give in and change your mind. They'll try to test your resolve. Don't give in! Unless he stops singing "Freebird" and starts humming "I Will Always Love You," you must be willing to pack your bags and walk.

ROMANTIC RULE: *During a negotiation, the person who wins is the person who is also willing to lose.*

The person who is willing to leave an unworkable situation always has the power. So don't give yours up. He must understand that you aren't going to give up on your life goals, and that this is not a ploy. He'll have no reason to take you seriously if you abandon yourself, cave in, and allow yourself to agree to a No-Time-Frame-Dating arrangement. Don't return to the status quo. Make your request, set a boundary, and then quickly Cover the Cage. Don't take his calls or respond to his e-mails or text messages. Let him sweat it out, and hopefully figure it out!

MANHANDLING TIP: *Don't reward men who are ambivalent about stepping up by continuing to talk to them, date them, or sleep with them!*

Step 5. The Bargaining Phase

He may try to stall for time by saying that he wants to (get engaged, have a baby, marry you, move in together, buy a home, have a future), but not this very second, and make seductive pleas like "Baby, you'll get everything you want if you just hang in there!" and "Relax! We're on the marriage track." Allow this to fall on deaf ears.

MAN FACT: *Male Language Decoder:* At this point, the words "maybe" and "hang in there" mean "No!"

Step 6. Let Him Brood

The next three months will be agonizing but well worth the pain and trouble. Suck it up, sister! Shut him down. (Cry all about town, and have hot rebound sex if you wish. It's delish!) Keep your commitment to yourself and leave him in the dust. This is often the only way to stimulate the feeling (courage) that most males need to voluntarily fly into the relationship cage and nest with you.

Hopefully, your departure will engender the following responses in him: grief, misery, craziness, loss of appetite, tearing of hair, inability to sleep, and feeling like he's been thrown into a pit of despair.

If you are patient, he may wind up crying on your doorstep at 3 A.M. and actually propose!

Amazing Fact: You can't lose either way! If he flies south, he was just holding up traffic and you've wisely set yourself free to find a true Lovebird. You've just killed two birds with one stone! But if he comes back with his hand on his heart, and is now ready to pledge allegiance to your flag, you'll be well rewarded for your expert troubles.

Result: The eagle has landed!

The Phoenix

Sometimes fate takes a strange turn. The man who flew south, the same one you were sure was gone for good, suddenly pops right back into your life. You never saw it coming, but there he is on the other end of the line, or on your doorstep, or at your college reunion, and he still looks *hot!* Ohmygod.

He confesses that he's missed you after all these years (months, weeks, or days—whenever you gave him the boot), and he swears that he's finally grown up. He's ready to step up . . . and begs you to give him one more try . . . and then he kisses you and positively insists that you do!

You don't need my advice about how to handle this rare bird . . . I think you can probably figure this one out all by yourself. He's transformed himself from a raging Bat Out of Hell into the Bluebird of Happiness.

And by the way . . . congratulations! Feel free to send me an invitation. I probably won't be able to make it, but I promise to send you a *lovely* card.

And hand in hand by the edge of the sand
They danced by the light of the moon,
The moon,
The moon,
They danced by the light of the moon.

-"The Owl and the Pussycat"

The Aviary

This comprehensive Birding Guide will help you identify the bachelors who are winging around your neighborhood. Once you decide who your Target Birds are, and can spot them with ease, you'll never again mistake rabid avifauna for the wonderful birds that are in full view!

The Albatross

This divorced dad has a brood and an angry ex hanging around his neck. And now he's hanging on to yours for dear life! *Warning:* If he hates his ex, it'll be like going into a wartorn country and trying to stage a love-in. You'll get undermined and probably nuked.

Habitats: Soccer practice, Toys 'R' Us, school plays, family therapy, Yahoo personals.

Song: "All By Myself."

Plumage: Khakis, Hawaiian shirts, and terrible lace-up shoes, all jumbled in the closet of his crappy rental apartment.

Mating Habits: Desperate. Needy, grabby. May cry before, dur-

227

ing, or after sex. *Beware:* Hot dates often get derailed by little people, so bring a turtleneck.

Care and Feeding Tips: Bring Kleenex and practice sympathetic phrases like "Umm-hmm, how awful. There, there." You won't even need to wax to perk him up 'cause his ex refused to have sex with him years ago and he's all backed up.

The Arctic Tern

Something traumatic must have happened at boarding school or while in foster care to cause his total emotional lockdown. This is one bird who is never defrosting.

Habitats: Uptown, downtown, all around the town.

Song: "Cold as Ice."

Plumage: Brooks Brothers shirts or an orange jumpsuit. May have roman numerals after his name on business card or on his rap sheet.

Mating Habits: Has his secretary (or parole officer) schedule dates for him. Wear a muffler.

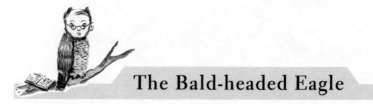

The Bald-headed Eagle

This classic May/December romance with Svengali is perfect for a perky Lolita who needs a little therapy (well, maybe a lot of therapy, but I'm not judging).

Habitats: College campus, college bars, strip clubs . . . jail!

Song: "Thank Heaven for Little Girls."

Markings: Bald. Says embarrassing things in front of your friends, like *"I'm ready to rock the house"* and *"Those pimp daddies shizzle my mcnizzle!"*

Mating Habits: Bossy, controlling, and pervy, in a *very* good or completely pathetic kind of way.

Care and Feeding Tips: Slip into your Catholic schoolgirl uniform and Mary Janes. Warning: Avoid the ex-wife. She'll be about as happy to see you as crow's-feet.

The Bat Out of Hell

Irresistible to anyone who's ever ovulated, this charismatic sex genius has so many exes' names tattooed on him, he's running out of room! This devastatingly handsome bad boy is hot and he knows it.

Habitats: Dark recording studios, tour bus, strip clubs, your knickers.

Song: "I Want You to Want Me."

Markings: Sexual atheism.

Mating Habits: Anything that will put you over the edge.

Care and Feeding: This species soars over open country in search of its main source of entertainment: groupie girls. So hit your knees and give him what he wants—applause, applause, applause. Good night, Cleveland!

The Bird of Paradise

This hot vacation romance is the adult version of the summer love you had at fourteen when tongue kissing was still *totally gross!* He's too hot for you and you both know it. *Tip:* Hide your purse.

Habitats: Not America! Cabanas, Club Med vacations, ancient ruins, gazebos, turrets.

Song: You never heard it before, can't understand a word of it, but it's soooo catchy.

Markings: Has accent and a tan, smells like foreign tobacco, cocoa butter, and strange exotic spices. Often has unfortunate body odor, too.

Mating Habits: Warning: May suddenly propose. Do not succumb! Leave this Bird of Paradise where you found him and when you're done, fly far, far away.

Care and Feeding Tips: Lie back and enjoy the ride . . . until he steals your heart (and your jewelry).

The Bluebird of Happiness

You've given up hope of ever finding your prince when all of a sudden, *bam!* Sometimes dreams really do come true.

Habitats: It's a mystery. The Lords of Karma will decide.

Song: "Some Enchanted Evening."

Plumage: Knows how to match his clothing but not in a gay way.

Mating Habits: Sweeps you right off your feet and into his arms.

Care and Feeding Tips: Something old, something new, something borrowed, something blue.

The Blue Jay

This A-type go-getter is in the market for a luxury car and the right woman to buckle into his passenger seat. Learn how to make the perfect martini and climb up the corporate ladder with Mr. Wanna B. Trump.

Habitats: Chatting up investors in business class, country clubs, and smoky cigar bars.

Song: "Life in the Fast Lane."

Plumage: Armani suit and Prada shoes. You can wax his Beamer with all the hair gel he's sporting. Scent: Hypnotique and Pure Ambition!

Mating Habits: Flashy! Impresses you with bottles of wine that he can't pronounce but orders with confidence, and rosy talk of the future . . .

Care and Feeding Tips: What might've been a buy at 10 A.M. can be a sell before the closing bell. So beware: He may not hold his position overnight! To be a long-term investment, show him your assets.

The Bushtit*

This man needs to make up his mind. He's insatiably drawn to T&A, on you and on everyone else, too! At first, you will find him a delight, and then an *incredible* pest. He also may suffer from Sexual A.D.D. and Sexual O.C.D. and have outstanding warrants at the DMV.*

Habitats: Where don't you find him? He's everywhere.

Song: "Super Freak."

Markings: He'll spot you first. He could be posing as anything, *even an accountant or a dentist!* Check for carpal tunnel of the wrist.

Mating Habits: Whenever he can get it.

Care and Feeding Tips: Work the pole and then look the other way in blissful denial, or immediately hire a private dick. Better yet, why not dump the Bushtit, and find a nice private dick you can have all to yourself?

* Sadly, I did not make this bird up! I'm a Ph.DD. and have a (terrible) reputation to maintain. So feel free to Google the Bushtit if you want to. You'll find that you owe me a little apology, but I'll be happy to forgive you.

The Cardinal

Jesus freak.

Habitats: Bible study, prayer groups, Amy Grant/ Michael W. Smith concerts, and in the aisle testifying!

Song: "Your Own Personal Jesus."

Markings: Rosy glow, everything on him is ironed and creased, and his best friend is Jesus.

Mating Habits: Not until marriage, silly! And then get ready for the missionary position.

Care and Feeding Tips: Don't cuss. Say, *"I love the Lord!"* *"Thank you, Jesus!"* and whip up a peach cobbler for the bake sale.

The Chicken

This garden-variety commitment-phobe would rather drown in the rain than get back in the barn.

Habitats: You're not quite sure because he's flown the coop!

Song: "Freebird."

Markings: Ring-finger amputee.

Mating Habits: Hot 'n' heavy until you ask where your relationship is going . . . then just sit back and watch him run around in circles.

Care and Feeding Tips: Slice up carrots and celery and put on a pot of water. Add salt, then lure Chicken into the henhouse. Slam door!

The Clay Pigeon

This amazing pest won't take the hint and buzz off. Clay pigeons get shot down in every gin joint in town.

Habitats: Blocking the view of the cute boy who's standing right behind him.

Song: "Do You Really Want To Hurt Me?"

Plumage: Whatever was in vogue five years ago, and cheap shoes.

Mating Habits: Says, *"Haven't I met you somewhere before?" "Do you come here often?" "Smile."*

Care and Feeding Tips: Pull, then shoot!

The Cockatoo

These guys are bona fide sex symbols, aka athletes, movie stars, and underwear models. They need approval, and need to get it *everywhere!* And they do, they most certainly do, whether clothed or naked.

Habitats: On set, on the tour bus, at the hottest bar in town.

Plumage: Free designer duds or selections from their own clothing label. Bling and chinchilla and a Hummer, too.

Song: "I'm Too Sexy."

Mating Habits: When he says he's playing nine holes, he doesn't mean golf.

Care and Feeding Tips: Assume the position and worship. Then pop some gum and ask for an autograph for your mom. *Note*: You may need to assume the position again for good measure.

The Condor

He's flying high in the rarefied atmosphere of his exceptional fame, fortune, power, or prestige. Your garden-variety rock star or financial wizard. *Warning:* You'll have to survive the Dreaded Entourage of exes, kids, publicists, fans, and hot-stone massage therapists while trying to bag this big boy.

Habitats: The offices of his divorce attorney, his business manager, and his shrink, or in the limo. Actually, you have no damned clue. He could be anywhere and his assistants are paid to skillfully cover his tracks.

Song: "Goldfinger."

Markings: Ink on his hands (from signing contracts and autographs), a photo-op smile, and tons of loot to boot.

Mating Habits: He's so used to being taken care of that he may be lazy in the sack . . . but you'll have tons of fun with the gardener!

Care and Feeding Tips: Surrounds himself with an entourage of parasites on the payroll, so the trick here is to figure out what you have to offer that the rest of the posse doesn't *Tip:* It probably rhymes with "Snow Job" or "Fanal Kex."

The Coot

He's as old as the hills and estranged from the rightful heirs to his estate and sizable fortune (*see* Anna Nicole).

Habitats: Early bird special, intensive care, rest homes, but he's on wheels so he could be anywhere. In winter, see large groups of Coots migrating to Florida.

Song: "Knockin' on Heaven's Door."

Markings: Liver spots and a schoolboy grin.

Mating Habits: He can't anymore, so bring a book. You can have him tucked under the covers by 8:00 and be on top of your lover by 8:09.

Care and Feeding Tips: Wear rubber-soled flats and a nurse's outfit. Put his head between your breasts and wiggle to make him giggle.

The Crowing Cock

It's all he can think about!

Habitats: Internet chat rooms using the handle 9"4U. (He's often delusional too!)

Song: "You Were Always on My Mind."

Markings: Male.

Care and Feeding: Lie. Say, *"Ohmygod you're huge!"* and *"Of course I came!"*

The Cuckoo Bird

Master of the double message. He makes even the most confident women want to pop out of a clock from his on-again, off-again behavior.

Habitats: At his other girlfriend's house.

Song: "Hello, Goodbye."

Markings: Wedding-ring tan line.

Mating Habits: *He'll* call *you* (because he keeps changing his number).

Care and Feeding Tips: Take him to couples counseling and watch the feathers fly!

The Dirty Bird

You wonder where all your panties are. Newsflash! *He's wearing them!* Has an assortment of punishments for bad behavior, none of which you'll want to miss.

Habitats: Your back door, dungeons, porn sites, and orgies, oh my!

Song: "Walk on the Wild Side."

Plumage: Leather and a whip, or a collar and leash!

Care and Feeding Tips: Say, *"Yes, master!"* or *"Down boy!"*

The Dodo Bird

This hot jock's good with his tools, but he's a very poor speller. Who cares? When he asks you to hand him the "duck tape," just tell him to take his shirt off and move your furniture around. Looking at him is like taking a little vacation . . . until he speaks. Well, I guess all good things must come to an end, must come, must come . . . ummm . . . what was I saying?

Habitats: Home Depot, GED classes for recidivists, and the gym.

Song: "Do You Think I'm Sexy?"

Plumage: He's always in workout clothes, but you prefer to see him naked!

Mating Habits: Likes dating clients and fixing their pipes, too!

Care and Feeding Tips: Say, *"Do you have a condom in your toolbox?"* See Jaybird.

The Dove

He's always strapped for cash but you don't give a hoot because he makes you feel like Juliet. The perfect choice for a power diva with her IRAs in order, or idealistic college girls on allowance.

Habitats: *Your* place (your dorm, your couch, and between your thighs!).

Song: "The Air That I Breathe."

Plumage: Thrift-shop chic. Bed-head haircut and pushing his beater off to the side of the road.

Mating Habits: Love letters, handwritten poems, flowers pulled from the park, and a devilish spark.

Care and Feeding Tips: Remember to feed him! He's *always* hungry. And don't let him chip in, because he needs the gas money.

The Falcon

This fetishist can be domesticated but only through rigorous training.

Habitats: Your arm.

Song: "Unchain My Heart."

Plumage: Bondage gear.

Mating Habits: Very loyal and attentive once tamed.

Care and Feeding Tips: Buy sexy leather gloves, blindfold him, and tell him to call you "Mistress." Then give him a smack.

The Fledgling

The perfect afternoon snack. This boy is a delight and your very own after-school special, but play it safe and make him pull out his ID first.

Habitats: The mall, the arcade, mowing your lawn, and then trimming your bushes.

Song: "Mama Told Me (Not To Come)."

Plumage: Peach fuzz, baby fat, priapic condition in his pants.

Mating Habits: Until you say, *"You've got to go now, my husband will be home any minute."* He's got energy to burn and is consistent. Say, *"See you next Tuesday at the ice cream parlor."*

Care and Feeding: Feed him Pop-Tarts while you're dressed in lingerie.

The Harpee Eagle

This most powerful bird of prey flies up to 60 mph through dense jungle, then swoops in and carries you off to Des Moines. Now you're planning the wedding and you don't even remember dating.

Habitats: Wherever you are.

Song: "Sign, Sealed, Delivered."

Plumage: Drives a U-Haul, has extra set of keys.

Mating Habits: You'll be taking conversion class before you know it.

Care and Feeding Tips: Be prepared to "come to" in a couple of months, so just sublet your apartment; don't give up the lease!

The Hawk

He's got a penchant for law and order, so shape up and take orders from Sarge.

Habitats: Gun range, the B&D section of the sex shop, Republican conventions, police stations (on the right side of the desk!), Neighborhood Watch, vigilante groups, and church.

Song: "Battle Hymn of the Republic" and "I Love This Bar."

Plumage: Buzz cut, sunburned neck, aviator sunglasses, Cadillac four-door sedan with trunk space for firearms—if it isn't already filled with them.

Mating Habits: Barks orders from his Barcalounger, discusses Fox news alerts with intensity.

Care and Feeding Tips: Keep meat treats and beer on hand and say, *"Yes, sir. Would you like another?"* and he'll be saluting *you* in no time!

The Homing Pigeon

Homer will want you to burn your little black book and Hop on Pop. He's ready to roost, so don't be surprised when he hits his knees on your six-month anniversary, which he'll remember, plan for, and remind *you* about. If you're on the fence, beware! He'll be roosting with another by the time you get your ass into therapy and realize that the only way to work out your fear of commitment is to *make one*.

Habitats: On the prowl at the jewelry store, and on bended knee.

Song: "Going to the Chapel."

Plumage: Just bought his first house and has ample closet space.

Mating Habits: Romantic dinners and meetings with the preacher.

Care and Feeding Tips: Say, *"Yes."*

The Horned Owl

This brainy nerd may not fit your *GQ* fantasy, but he'll *rock your nation* with his deeply passionate nature. He'll give you multiple orgasms, diagram them to explain their inner workings, and warble an aria for you at the end of your dream date.

Habitats: Lectures on campus, environmental protests, poetry readings, synagogue, bookstores, libraries, and the opera!

Song: "She Blinded Me with Science."

Plumage: Tweed, plaid, khakis, glasses. His outfit may be ill-fitting, but his binary code is *perfect.*

Mating Habits: Caught your eye on Nerve—or was it Match—with the only good picture *ever* taken of him. Quotes Plato's *Republic,* but one night in his bed might make you feel like you're at Plato's *Retreat.*

Care and Feeding Tips: Act like you're listening. Say, *"Wow, that is fascinating!"* *"How does fusion work again?"* Or a simple *"Yes"* will do.

The Ivory-Billed Woodpecker

You thought you were happily married, but when you see him at your reunion, he gives you a romantic flashback.

Habitats: High school and college reunions and walks down memory lane. If that doesn't work, Google him.

Song: "Reunited."

Plumage: Surrounded by that golden glow from the past and wearing your favorite cologne.

Care and Feeding Tips: Reverie. Illicit affairs while you're at home visiting the folks. *Tip:* reread your high school diary so you remember why you dumped him in the first place!

The Jailbird

He's incarcerated but you still love him. *Aversion therapy:* Watch reruns of *Oz*.

Habitats: Lockdown, prison laundry room, the yard.

Song: "Thirty Days in the Hole."

Markings: Prison tats, scars, gunshot wounds, and a body just this side of heaven.

Mating Habits: The prison kiss: hands raised up against the glass. He's also mastered the five-minute conjugal visit. *Warning:* Don't bring up anal; he'll take it the wrong way.

Care and Feeding Tips: A cake with a file inside it. Duh!

The Jaybird

This chipper fellow is fantastic in the bedroom but embarrassing at your parents' anniversary party.

Habitats: Nude beaches, trench coats, nudist colonies.

Song: "Whoomp! (There It Is)."

Markings: No tan lines!

Mating Habits: Anytime, anywhere, as long as it's inappropriate.

Care and Feeding Tips: SPF 40 and forget to wear panties!

The Lark

As in: "I have no idea why I slept with him . . . it was just a lark!"

Habitats: Cancun, Vegas, Daytona Beach, and Miami. Any local nightclub will do. Or try the DMV, the podiatrist, the grocery store . . . this bird can be spotted just about anywhere.

Song: "Why Don't We Get Drunk and Screw."

Plumage: You were way too drunk and it was way too dark, but you seem to remember he had nice white teeth.

Mating Habits: Fast! Pickup line: *"Do you live around here? My truck is right out back and it's all gassed up."*

Care and Feeding Tips: You don't remember but it certainly did the trick!

The Loon

What woman hasn't fallen in love, at least once, with a manic man who suddenly plummets into a catatonic depression?

Habitats: Rehab, lockdown, the pharmacy, your bushes.

Song: "Crazy."

Plumage: Wild eyes, dark circles, and four-day stubble.

Mating Habits: Intense and dangerously spontaneous. Shows up at your door at 4 A.M. unannounced, laughing or crying, or crying and laughing.

Care and Feeding Tips: Drive your Loon to the ASPCA and put him on meds. Sorry, I meant drive this sick pup to the doctor ASAP. (*I need a massage.*)

The Lovebird

Will die of loneliness if not kept in pairs!

Habitats: The funeral home, bereavement groups, the obituaries, online at www.greyfoxes.com.

Song: "I Will Always Love You."

Plumage: Love in his eyes.

Mating Habits: Wife Number 1, Wife Number 2 . . . then you!

Care and Feeding Tips: Bring a brisket to the shiva and casserole to the wake.

The Master Cock

He's the ultimate lover!

Habitats: Lakers games, hip-hop functions, and Jacob the jeweler.

Song: "Magic Stick."

Plumage: Anaconda in the boxers. Sean Jean velour jogging suit, Rolex (could be fake), large diamond in left ear, Escalade, Hummer, or Benz, oh my.

Mating Habits: Cristal, late nights of dancing, and weed. Says irresistible things like *"Baby, you looking kinda skinny!"*

Care and Feeding Tips: Bend over while you're wearing a thong.

The Mockingbird

When you ask him if you look fat, he says, *"Yes."* Then when you get upset, he says you're being sensitive and that he was just joking.

Habitats: Perched on a branch right above you.

Song: "Kim."

Plumage: Perpetual sneer, beady eyes, and unattractive on the *inside*.

Mating Habits: Premature ejaculator . . . *ewwww!*

Care and Feeding Tips: Drop him! Start doing affirmations, go to karate, and change your locks. And then pick up a Master Cock!

The Mynah Bird

This was an insignificant love affair and now you can't get rid of him.

Habitats: Virtually everywhere—your voice mail, your e-mail, and in your shadow.

Song: "I Want You to Want Me."

Plumage: Wears the sweater you bought him every day to show how much he cares.

Mating Habits: Total cling-on and deliberately obtuse.

Care and Feeding Tips: Deny him to inspire his desire. He takes rejection fabulously!

The Nightingale

This honey-tongued smooth talker sings your praises but develops a case of permanent laryngitis when it comes to making a commitment.

Habitats: Your boudoir.

Song: "Smooth Operator."

Plumage: Twelve-year-old blended Scotch, multiple exes, a luxury sports car, and *you*. And then *her*. And then maybe you again if you fall for him a second time! Please read Secret Male Lemon Law Disclaimer on page 63.

Mating Habits: Has more lines than a Colombian drug lord. Wines you and dines you, and then shines you on . . . until he calls again.

Care and Feeding Tips: Denial. *Yours* and then *his!*

The Nuthatch

Beware a man better groomed and prettier than you! How to tell if this guy's a model/actor or just . . . gay. *Bonus tip:* "Bisexual" also just means . . . gay.

Habitats: Jamba Juice, the gym, Armani Exchange, the mirror.

Song: "Beautiful."

Markings: Killer body and dazzling teeth.

Mating Habits: Picks you up at the gym where he can inspect your abs before he strips you butt naked. Smokers need not apply.

Care and Feeding Tips: To find out if he's bi, say, *"Who designed those pants? They're fabulous!"*

The Ostrich

He won't understand why you were so upset when you found his ex-girlfriend's diaphragm in the medicine chest while you were innocently looking for . . . his ex-girlfriend's diaphragm. You'll want to hit him on the head with an iron, but even that won't make an impression, and now he'll be unconscious for real.

Habitats: Deep in de-Nile.

Song: "It Wasn't Me."

Markings: Sand in his bed.

Mating Habits: Changing the subject.

Care and Feeding Tips: Make excuses *for* him. Excellent match for a woman with poor confrontational skills, or a spy . . . then you can both pretend that nothing is happening, *together.*

The Parrot

This one's a lifer. Says whatever you want to hear and has mastered the difficult phrase "Yes, dear."

Habitats: You can leave the cage door open and he won't fly away!

Song: "Someone to Watch over Me."

Plumage: Wedding band.

Mating Habits: However you want it, and whenever you'll let him have it.

Care and Feeding Tips: He's completely trained and won't drink from the carton.

A Partridge in a Pear Tree

A holiday hookup between Thanksgiving and New Year's, or the desperate Valentine's Day date when you were lonely, or tipsy, or both. This is one mercy shag where you're feeling sorry for the both of you!

Habitats: Under the mistletoe.

Song: "It's Beginning to Look a Lot Like Christmas."

Markings: So not your type, you can't even pretend this has a chance. The romantic spirit is out on the curb the next week, along with the tree.

Mating Habits: Do you really care? I didn't think so!

Care and Feeding Tips: Say, *"Would you like some eggnog? And then a snog?"*

The Peacock
(Un-gay version of the Nuthatch)

This preening Don Juan needs to have all eyes on him, at all times. His femmy self-involvement is way beyond metrosexual. He's a label whore and will tell you how much he spent on his Prada loafers. Always irritatingly well-groomed, he'll eye you over to check out the competition!

Habitats: The chair (dentists, hair dressers, facialists).

Song: "You're So Vain."

Markings: Pinky ring, alligator shoes, wearing more jewelry than you.

Mating Habits: Flashes gorgeous grin and says, *"I love your shoes."*

Care and Feeding Tips: Always carry a compact mirror and say things like *"Wow, your ass looks amazing in those Gucci pants!"* Dress down so as not to upstage him. This Peacock often likes a drab little Wren for a consort.

The Penguin

He's monogamous, mates for life, and is already dressed for the wedding.

Habitats: Other people's weddings, singles' mixers, speed dating, Match.com.

Song: "Lady in Red."

Plumage: Southern drawl or British accent, empty ring finger, tux at the ready, and a bike rack built for two.

Mating Habits: He's fast! Better first-date interrogator than you are. Has the pastor on speed dial. He's a bobsled of love and he wants to go cross-country with you. *See* Stork.

Care and Feeding Tips: Say, "*I'd be honored to be Mrs. [Whatever his last name is]*" . . . and then make him a highball and rumaki!

The Pigeon

This rat with wings keeps crapping all over you.

Habitats: Your ATM card, your couch, your car, and after you kick him out, her ATM, her couch, her car.

Song: "Just a Gigolo."

Plumage: Whatever you bought for him.

Mating Habits: Ask him to shower before 'cause he's dirty!

Care and Feeding Tips: Crumbs! Don't overfeed or he'll definitely take advantage. *Tip:* Put your valuables in the wall safe.

The Pink Flamingo

The Flamingo monopolizes all of your time, but he's hard to resist because he's the Best Boyfriend Ever! And girlfriend, too.

Habitats: Your mirror, your closet (where you catch him trying to jam his big feet into your designer shoes). Or on the dance floor at The Manhole and The Mineshaft.

Song: "Wind Beneath My Wings" (remix).

Plumage: Anything more expensive than what you're wearing.

Mating Habits: He'll hate your ex as much as you do . . . and want the make-up sex just as badly! Don't fall in love with him or you so *won't* be screwed.

249

Care and Feeding Tips: A fashion crisis, celebrity gossip, and boy trouble. To snag him, say *"Want to rent Beaches and have a cuddle? We can paint each other's toes and not have sex!"*

The Raven

Heartbroken and pacing your living room floor,

And completely obsessed with an ex named Lenore,

Save yourself the aggravation and show him the door.

Your romantic prognosis: Nevermore!! Nevermore!!

The Roadrunner

Comes on hot and heavy, then drops you right where he found you.

Habitats: Route 66.

Song: "On the Road Again."

Plumage: It's a blur, he moved too fast.

Mating Habits: Wham bam, thank you, ma'am!

Care and Feeding Tips: Remember to leave the door open. On second thought, forget it. He'll just fly out the window.

The Robin Redbreast

You just love him, and so do all of his ex-girlfriends, his mother, his yoga instructor, and even, you suspect, some of his guy friends . . . 'cause let's face it, he's Prince Charming. Sometimes dreams really do come true!

Plumage: Baseball cap, smile lines, and a tan from doing yard work.

Habitats: The park, the Y, or his mom's kitchen flipping burgers for the entire family.

Song: "Close to You."

Mating Habits: Will romance you at barbecues, sports bars, your local park, and in lover's lane after dark.

Care and Feeding Tips: Learn how to share your toys if sweet Robin wants to roost with you. He really is the boy wonder!

The Rubber Ducky

This is one birdie that's made to order!

Habitats: Your nightstand drawer.

Song: "I Touch Myself."

Markings: Comes in a variety of colors and sizes, both plastic and rubber.

Care and Feeding: Triple A's or an extension cord will do. Shake a tail feather, baby!

The Scrub Jay

This adulterous bird is an unrepentant freeloader. All he's got to offer is his tremendous appendage and pimp-style mind control.

Habitats: His caddy, the track, the corner.

Song: "I Put a Spell On You."

Markings: He's always suited and booted in swank Gators, Playa chalice, and bejeweled pimp hand.

Mating Habits: The bitch slap.

Care and Feeding Tips: Just bring him the money, honey!

The Sparrow

Accountants and dentists. This is no glamour mating, but you may accidentally fall deeply in love with his codependent tendencies and your newly balanced checkbook.

Habitats: Online, his parents' house, and blind dates . . . everyone always tries to help the Sparrow out because they know he needs an assist. It's a mitzvah!

Song: "My Guy."

Plumage: Volvo or Saab if he's sporty, polo shirts, pressed pants, and the all-important pocket protector.

Mating Habits: Sincere and (yawn) boring. But your mother will be thrilled.

Care and Feeding Tips: Smile.

The Stork

He wants to spread his seed. The Stork can be the most dangerous bird of 'em all. He'll sidetrack your dreams, your ambition, and your career with one sabotaged condom! Often this is the reformed bachelor in his forties who meets a *hot* twenty-something and knows that this time, it's the real thing. Again. Only this time he's actually ready.

Habitats: Lamaze classes, Planned Parenthood, Babies 'R' Us.

Plumage: Has stroller in the trunk, and more baby mammas than an NBA player.

Song: "Papa Don't Preach."

Mating Habits: Won't want to keep his Trojan on.

Care and Feeding Tips: Ovulate.

The Toucan

If he can put it up his bill, he will. This fruit loop is a jet-set party boy!

Habitats: Fashion shows, yachts, Botega Veneta, the A-list.

Song: "White Lines."

Mating Habits: Says, *"Want a bump?" "Are you a model?"*

Plumage: Maserati, Bentley, and anything really expensive that still looks cheap and shiny.

Care and Feeding Tips: Keep the following in your purse: your passport, a bikini bottom, a razor blade, and a mirror.

The Turkey

Opens his car door first when it's raining or says, *"Yes"* when you ask if he'd like you to "chip in" when the check comes. He'll even watch you struggle with your luggage! He's CHEEP and lazy.

Habitats: KFC, drive-throughs, and fine mall dining.

Song: "If I Only Had a Brain."

Plumage: Belly jelly, stains on shirts, sandals with socks.

Mating Habits: Quotes *The Simpsons*. Dream dates include Sizzler, drive-throughs, strange international foods found in strip malls.

Care and Feeding Tips: Doughnuts and fried foods. Fresh batteries for remote or vibrator, because he's way too lazy to entertain you.

The Turtledove

He's so sweet that even though he's allergic to kittens, he's doesn't want to hurt their feelings, so he pets them with mittens!

Habitats: His place. Online with a pseudonym, late-night bookstores, the pharmacy (tends toward hypochondria), or tucked into a quiet corner of the library.

Song: "Creep."

Plumage: Sunglasses, Purell, and cigarettes. When nervous has a cute little stutter.

Mating Habits: You'll have to make the first move, so be prepared to be shot down several times before he consents. He may totally blow your mind in the bedroom, so be patient, he's worth it.

254

Care and Feeding Tips: Coax him out of his shell and into your bedroom slowly. *Tip*: No sudden movements. He's easily startled!

The Ugly Duckling

He's so not your type, but when you give him a chance, he magically turns into a swan.

Habitats: Whenever and wherever you need him.

Song: "My Funny Valentine."

Markings: Ugly, and then actually quite handsome.

Care and Feeding Tips: A closer look.

The Vampire Bat

This bloodsucker will charm you, but once you're under his spell, he will drain you as dry as the Sahara. This man is into power and needs to diminish yours to feel better about himself. This can range from mere psychological abuse to financial demands or even violence. Save yourself! Eat Italian and grab a crucifix and quickly drive a stake through the relationship's heart. If that doesn't work, call my cousin Tony and ask him to pay the bloodsucker a visit!

Habitats: The dark side.

Song: "Under My Thumb."

Markings: Seductive ways soon give way to foul temper and a permanent scowl.

Mating Habits: This Prince Charming turns into Attila the Hun, and then magically reappears again when your bags are packed.

Care and Feeding Tips: Therapy and a Taser.

The Vulture

He has no shame and will try to pick you up at a funeral, the police station, or a self-help group. This opportunistic predator has no conscience. He prefers wounded prey who are too distracted by grief to put up much resistance.

Habitats: Funerals, police stations, court, cruising self-help groups.

Song: "Lean On Me."

Plumage: Carries Kleenex, matches, and a bail bondsman's number.

Mating Habits: Says, *"Let me buy you a cup of coffee." "Tell me all about it."*

Care and Feeding Tips: Sniffle. Bring a sob story and wipe your tears on his sleeve.

The White Pelican

Overweight middle-aged white man.

Habitats: Jazz fests, steak houses, pretending to be on the treadmill, not pedaling a stationary bike, sofa in the TV room, heavy metal reunions.

Song: Anything by Weird Al Yankovich and "Born to Run."

Plumage: Belly hanging over his shorts, Teva sandals with socks, Hawaiian shirts, and pasty-white (hairy) legs (yick). Collects BBCs and visors, and wears them, even the embarrassing umbrella hat with beer funnel.

Mating Habits: The American Classic—dinner and a movie.

Care and Feeding Tips: Always wants another helping. Help him correctly button up his (rumpled) shirt, and keep Gas-X handy!

The Wild Turkey

Your garden-variety lush.

Habitats: The bar, the package store, the floor.

Song: "Margaritaville."

Plumage: Bloodshot eyes and boozy breath.

Mating Habits: Oh, jeez, just get him off me! He's passed out midflight!

Care and Feeding Tips: You'll be the other woman to the bottle, the coke vial, or the beer can. *Tip:* The Wild Turkey's probably not for you, unless you love being a barfly, too.

The Woodpecker

Stays rock hard all the time! He'll rock your nation and make you pledge allegiance to his flag.

Habitats: The bedroom floor, the bathtub, the kitchen counter, the dining room tabletop, up against the wall in the foyer, the elevator . . . whoops! We're back in the foyer again . . .

Song: "Dr. Feelgood."

Plumage: A permanent stiffy, encased in tight underwear (for control).

Mating Habits: Drills the hole anytime, anyplace; your neighbors are registering official complaints because of noisy banging in the wee hours.

Care and Feeding Tips: Lube and a towel.

The Wounded Bird

He has more issues than a magazine kiosk. This guy will suck you drier than a bone in the desert and suspect *you're* the one who needs professional help for *even thinking* that you could rehabilitate him.

Habitats: Your shoulder, the self-help section in the bookstore, lying on the train tracks.

Song: "Love Hurts."

Markings: Tear-stained cheeks, empty bottle of Prozac chased by half a bottle of rum.

Mating Habits: Cries *before* sex.

Care and Feeding Tips: Feed him something with a backbone.

about the author

Lauren Frances, Ph.DD, has spent countless hours of exhausting (but deeply gratifying) undercover research perfecting her man-wrangling techniques. She has appeared on Extra, VH1, and talk radio as a leading sexpert in her field. She is the founder of the Institute for Romantic Research, and her column, "The Hollywood Dating Food Chain," is published in *Flaunt* magazine. She lives in Los Angeles. Visit her website, www.LaurenFrances.net.

[Knock. Knock. Knock.]

"Scarlett? Are you in there? Open the door!"

"Is that you, Morris?"

"No! It's me, Rhett."

[Beat. Scarlett opens the door a crack.]

"My, you have a very high opinion of yourself, Captain Butler. What makes you think you can waltz right in and boss me around? Besides you've been just awful leaving me to fend for myself all these years. No. I don't think that I will."

[Scarlett slams the door shut!]

"I've been a fool. A damned idiot. . . . Scarlett, if you don't open this door, I'm going to break it down, and that'll hurt at my age. Please, Scarlett. [Softens.] *I've come to take you away, honey. . . . Marry me again . . . and this time, let's both* try *to be good."*

"Do you mean it, Rhett? Do you really? Oh, Rhett! You came back. You came back! I just knew that you would."

[She throws the door open, and Rhett smiles to himself with satisfaction. Scarlett has slipped into a very fetching dress . . . they fly into each other's arms.]

"I've come back to you and I'm never letting you go. And, Scarlett?"

"Yes, Rhett?"

"I don't want to hear another peep about Morris."

The End